Contract Drafting and Negotiation

for Entrepreneurs and Business Professionals

Paul A. Swegle

BLSG BUSINESS LAW
SEMINAR GROUP

Seattle, Washington

Library of Congress Control Number: 2018942264

eBook ASIN#: B07DM3J7B2
Paperback ISBN#: 978-0-692-13830-4

This book is dedicated to my wife Serena and to my children
Matthew and Stephanie.

Thank you Serena, Kurt Zumdieck, Jim Swegle and Johanna Fuhr for the unique
perspectives each of you provided in reviewing and editing my manuscript.

Contents

Introduction 1

    The Unforgiving Law of Contracts 1

    Hidden Hazards 2

    Leveraging the Business Mindset 2

    Perspective 3

    Caveats 3

Chapter One: CONTRACT LAW 5

    Contracts as Private Law 5

    Contract Formation 5

    Mutual Assent .6

    Authority 6

    Consideration .6

    Offer and Acceptance 7

    Defenses to Contract Formation 8

    The Parol Evidence Rule 10

    Exceptions to the Parol Evidence Rule 10

Promise versus Condition 12
Rules of Interpretation .13
Implied Covenant of Good Faith and Fair Dealing 15
Waiver, Modification 16
Letters of Intent and Oral Contracts 17
Breach, Damages and Remedies 20
Summary of Contract Law 23

Chapter Two: COMMON MISTAKES **25**

Performance before Agreement 25
Failing to Shop and Compare 27
Inadequate Descriptions of Performance Obligations 28
Weak or Nonexistent Remedies 29
Poor Vetting of Vendors, Suppliers and Others 31
Blindly Accepting "Standard Contracts" 31
Duration Too Long or Too Short 32
Poor Document Change Tracking and Proofing 32

Chapter Three: NEGOTIATION **33**

Negotiation Training 33
Demeanor and Attitude 34
Body Language 34
Get the Other Side Talking 34
Negotiating Chips 35
Do Not Negotiate Against Yourself 36
Conflicts of Interests .36
Protection of Confidential Information 37
Get Technical Documents and Specifications Early 38

Chapter Four: DRAFTING **39**

Clarity 39
Drafting Red Flags 40
Completeness 40
Technical Details 41

Understand the Deal 41

Active Analysis .42

Draft Marking 42

Initial Draft Issues 43

Handwritten Changes in Final Drafts 44

Chapter Five: COMMON CONTRACT TERMS 45

Introduction 45

Title/Caption 47

Opening Paragraph/Recitals/Background 48

Recitals or "Whereas" Clauses 48

Definitions 49

Obligations of the Parties/Services 50

Fees/Pricing/Fees and Payments 55

Intellectual Property/Proprietary Rights 57

Confidentiality/Confidential Information 63

Term and Termination 64

Effects of Termination 69

Remedies for Breach 72

Representations and Warranties 76

Disclaimers/Warranty Disclaimer 78

Limitations/Limitation of Liability 81

Indemnification 87

Insurance 94

Modification and Waiver 97

Arbitration 98

Severability 101

Assignment 103

Governing Law, Venue and Jurisdiction 105

Notices 108

Force Majeure 110

Entire Agreement/Integration/Merger 112

Legal Expenses/Legal Fees 112

Survival 113

Authority. 114

Counterparts 115

Signature Block 115

Chapter Six: IMPLEMENTATION **117**

Signing and Filing. 117

Tracking .118

Contract Management Technology 119

Performance 119

Deal Evolution 121

Chapter Seven: AMENDMENTS AND ADDENDUMS **123**

Changing Circumstances 123

Addendums 124

Amendments - Contract Surgery 124

Tactical Considerations 125

Consistency and Good Contract Management 125

Too Many Amendments 126

Chapter Eight: DISPUTE RESOLUTION **127**

Dispute Avoidance 127

Be Right 128

Keep Emotions in Check 128

Disputes are Just Difficult Negotiations 128

Initial Assessment. 129

Cats in Trees 130

Sand Traps 131

Code Red – Zero Sum Disputes 134

Use of Counsel 136

Introduction

The Unforgiving Law of Contracts

In 1990, a massive floating bridge between Seattle and Mercer Island used by thousands of cars every day sank in a storm while being refurbished. The state's agreement with the contractor was apparently unclear on who should pay for the sinking. After years of litigation, the contractor's insurers agreed to pay $20 million without admitting responsibility.

In 2013, Bertha, the largest and most expensive drill ever built, overheated and ground to a halt under Seattle. Again it was not clear who should pay the resulting repair and delay costs, estimated at one point to be $480 million.

In 2006, the Canadian Radio-television Telecommunications Commission weighed in on a very expensive punctuation dispute between Rogers Cable Communications and Aliant Telecom. The CRTC ruled that Aliant could terminate an agreement between the two parties much sooner than Rogers believed was permitted under the following passage:

> ... [the Structure Support Agreement] shall... continue in force for a period of five (5) years from the date it is made, and thereafter for successive five (5) year terms, unless and until terminated by one year prior notice in writing by either party.

Rogers had written the above passage intending that Aliant would not be able to terminate the agreement *until after the initial five year term.*

In its ruling, the CRTC found that placement of the comma before the phrase *"unless and until terminated by one year notice in writing by either party"* permitted *"termination of the SSA at any time, without cause, upon one year's written notice..."*

The CRTC's ruling allowed Aliant to terminate years earlier than Rogers had expected, apparently costing Rogers $2.4 million, all because of an errant comma.

Obviously, even professional contract negotiators and drafters miss important issues. Missteps like these happen both in government and in business. In business, cost constraints can limit access to competent legal counsel. Sometimes in high pressure business environments there is also pressure to act quickly and apologize later.

But commercial agreements are unforgiving. No apology will raise a sunken bridge, unwind an agreement that unexpectedly transfers your intellectual property, or otherwise re-write a deal that calls for the wrong goods or services or that spawns legal or regulatory liabilities.

Hidden Hazards

Unfortunately, many contract drafting traps are invisible to non-lawyers. It takes much less skill to critique what is *in* an agreement than it does to identify and correct what is *not* – things like remedies for breach, rights of termination, intellectual property protections, or correct descriptions of what the other party is supposed to do.

As a result, entrepreneurs and other business persons can overestimate their ability to competently negotiate commercial agreements without legal assistance. Sometimes this leads to painful surprises.

Leveraging the Business Mindset

On the other hand, entrepreneurs and other business persons with strong contract drafting and negotiation skills can be the most valuable individuals at the table. They often understand the economics and business logic of commercial relationships better than attorneys, and they usually take a more pragmatic and creative approach to finding the compromises needed to get deals done. And unlike counsel, who bring professional "malpractice" concerns to any project, sophisticated and well-informed business persons can be better positioned to weigh calculated risks regarding novel and complex commercial relationships.

Perspective

Most commercial agreements involve one party purchasing some type of good or service from another party, or a combination of goods and services. Thus, one party is often considered a "buyer," "customer" or "client," and the other a "seller," "vendor," "provider" or "supplier." For simplicity, we'll think in terms of buyers and sellers.

Many of the topics in this book are discussed largely from the perspective of the buyer. One reason for this is brevity. There are several others though.

- First, sellers often have standard contracts that they routinely present to buyers. In many cases, these standard contracts were drafted by the seller's lawyer months or years earlier and were loaded up with terms, both relevant and irrelevant, that favor the seller. Consequently, it is often the buyer who is faced with reviewing a new and potentially confusing agreement.

- Second, the buyer is often at an informational disadvantage. This is because sellers generally know more than their buyers about the goods or services being sold and about how to protect their interests in transactions involving those goods or services.

- Third, sellers might be slightly more apt to breach their commitments than buyers, given the generally more significant performance challenges facing sellers – e.g., producing and transporting goods on time, developing software on time, competently providing specialized services, and so forth.

In most contract situations, therefore, it is the buyer who needs more coaching on how to protect his or her interests. That said, where relevant, issues of particular importance from the seller's perspective are also addressed – e.g., developing solid but workable template agreements, avoiding over-promising, and limiting downside risk through warranty and liability limitation clauses, among others.

Keep perspective in mind and consider both sides of each issue. The ability to evaluate the other party's concerns is an advantage in contract negotiations, as discussed in Chapter Three, *Negotiation*.

Caveats

Nothing in this book is legal advice. Legal advice is always based on specific facts and requires an attorney-client relationship.

Also, this book also does not address the Uniform Commercial Code ("UCC") in detail. Article 2 of the UCC, adopted in varying forms by every state, applies to all contracts for "goods." Goods are defined as *any tangible thing that is moveable*. Readers who regularly buy or sell "goods" should work with counsel to ensure UCC issues are covered.

Chapter One

CONTRACT LAW

Contracts as Private Law

Contracts create "private law" between two parties. Courts enforce valid contracts in order to provide predictability in private relationships and to facilitate commerce. Enforceability is a double-edged sword though, rarely distinguishing between good deals and bad.

Throughout this book, there are references to "case law." Case law, also called "precedent," and "common law," means the general body of law created by state and federal courts of appeals.

Contract Formation

A contract is formed when there is "mutual assent" (also known as a "meeting of the minds") between two parties to enter into an agreement supported by "consideration" (money or something else given in exchange). Issues of "contract formation" are often relevant to a party seeking to get out of an agreement by arguing that a contract never occurred. We will consider what it takes to form a contract, and then several common "defenses" to contract formation, i.e., arguments that no contract was ever formed. Additional defenses to formation appear below in the discussion of the *Parol Evidence Rule*.

Mutual Assent

Mutual assent means that two parties over the age of "majority" (18 years) and of sound mind have *voluntarily* agreed to enter into an agreement under which each will do or provide certain things. Where fraud or duress is used to convince a party (i.e., gunpoint) to enter into an agreement, the requirement of voluntary assent is absent and the contract can be voided.

Interestingly, most contracts involving minors can be voided, but minors are generally not permitted to "disaffirm" contracts involving "necessities" like food, clothing and shelter.

Mutual assent can also be undermined by mutual mistake about a material fact or assumption, as discussed below under *Parol Evidence Rule*.

Authority

Another concept falling under "assent" is "authority" – the question of whether the individual signing for a party is actually authorized to enter into it on behalf of that party. Or, alternatively, has the other party held that person out as having such authority?

This should not be a concern where you are dealing directly with the president, chief financial officer, general counsel or sole proprietor of a company. But an unusually generous deal signed by a sales person or business development vice president, for example, might later be disputed as "unauthorized."

For any contract involving substantial risks, commitments or monetary value, consider demanding proof of actual authority. In the case of corporations or partnerships, this may involve requiring the other side to produce board resolutions, partnership operating agreements, or delegations of authority outlining the signing authorities of persons in certain positions.

Consideration

Each party has to agree to do or give something of value in exchange for the performance of the other party. If one party is not obligated to do or give anything of value, or their performance is otherwise voluntary or "illusory," there is no enforceable contract under law and *either* party may back out.

Even where the value of the consideration from one party is substantially greater than that from the other, courts generally do not intervene to invalidate such agreements. That said, contracts citing "$1" or "love and affection" in exchange for goods or services of measurably higher value might not survive attack in some states. The case law varies from one jurisdiction to another.

Courts in most states will not set aside a contract unless the "*inadequacy*" of one party's consideration "*is so gross as to be conclusive evidence of fraud and as to shock the conscience of the court.*" Cases where consideration is found to be wanting also usually involve other grounds for invalidation, such as fraud or duress.

It should be obvious from the above that gifts without consideration from the other party cannot be enforced under contract law.

Companies that fail to get proper intellectual property assignments at the time of hiring employees or contractors often stumble on this concept when they later try to get departed employees and independent contractors to sign intellectual property assignment forms without offering any consideration. Any such forms signed without some form of compensation are subject to being later disaffirmed by the former employee or contractor as unenforceable gifts. A document that would have had no price tag if signed at the beginning of an individual's employment can become much more costly when that employee knows that his or her signature is necessary to close a major financing or acquisition involving the former employer.

Offer and Acceptance

Although there have been cases involving questions of whether "offer and acceptance" to enter into an agreement truly occurred, such problems are rare and can be easily avoided. Use caution in making a proposal that might be viewed by the other party as a *firm offer* to enter into a contract. If you propose a sufficiently detailed arrangement, even orally, in a manner that could be reasonably interpreted as an offer to contract, acceptance by the other party can result in a binding contract – or at least a dispute to that effect.

To avoid such issues, lawyers often stamp draft agreements with "DRAFT PROPOSAL FOR DISCUSSION PURPOSES ONLY" or similar language.

Offer Termination

An offer that is detailed and definite enough to result in a contract if accepted is sometimes called a "firm offer." Once a firm offer has been made, it remains open until any of the following events:

- Rejection. If an offeree rejects an offer, or makes a counteroffer altering important terms, the offer is no longer open.

- Revocation. The offeror can revoke or retract an offer at any time before it is accepted, even if the offeror said or wrote that it would be open for a longer period. Sudden revocation of an outstanding offer may strike the offeree as unfair, but it is perfectly legal. Sitting on an offer carries risk of revocation without warning. Offerees can get around this concern by paying the offeror to keep the offer open. This is a separate contract itself, called an "option" – i.e., a contract allowing the offeree to make a decision about something later. Landlords, for example, are often willing to hold a space for a fee while a tenant takes an additional week or two to consider alternatives, giving the tenant and "option" on the space.

- ▪ Lapse. Some offers lapse at a stated time, and all offers are subject to termination after a "reasonable time" depending on the circumstances.

- ▪ Death. The death or insanity of the offeror will terminate an offer, as will the destruction of the subject matter of the offer.

Defenses to Contract Formation

Illegality

A contract must not require one or both parties to do something prohibited by law. If it does, all or part of the contract will be unenforceable, depending on the facts.

A contract to traffic in endangered species, for example, would be unenforceable between the parties, allowing either party to back out.

The same would be true of a contract to commit murder, fraud, or even a "tortious act" on a third party, including trespass, misrepresentation, defamation or contractual interference. Interestingly, amounts paid toward the performance of an illegal contract generally cannot be recovered in a civil lawsuit.

On the other hand, if a less important or secondary part of one party's performance requires an illegal act, for example improper collection or sharing of customer data, it becomes less clear that either party could simply walk away from the contract on the basis of illegality. A court would look at whether the contract contained a "severability" clause *(i.e., "If any part of this agreement is found unenforceable, it shall be deemed struck, without invalidating the remainder of the Agreement")* and whether the illegal requirement in the contract can simply be struck without undermining the overall intent of the parties.

Severability clauses are discussed further in Chapter Five, *Common Contract Terms.*

Against Public Policy

Even absent a specific rule or statute, a contract or a specific provision in a contract may be found by a court to be "against public policy." Depending on the circumstances, a court may invalidate all or part of the agreement or refuse to provide a remedy for breach of the agreement. Courts vary in how they define what is "against public policy," but the following statement from a New York court in 1991 is typical:

"An agreement is against public policy if it is injurious to the interests of the public, contravenes some established interest of society, violates some public statute, is against good morals, tends to interfere with the public welfare or safety, or is at war with the interests of society or in conflict with the morals of the time."

Public policy issues arise where there is an alleged public interest or impact beyond the narrow interests of two private parties. Not surprisingly, these concerns arise more often when a government, or "public," entity is party to a contract. For example, provisions in public works contracts requiring a municipality to indemnify (defend in court, pay fines, judgments, and so forth) a contractor for the contractor's own negligence (failure to use due care) have been invalidated as "against public policy."

Once such an argument has prevailed where a government entity is involved, it is possible for the precedent to be applied successfully between private litigants. The case law regarding provisions requiring a party to be indemnified for its own gross negligence or willful misconduct has followed this pattern.

As another example, public policy arguments have also been used to invalidate "unreasonable post-employment restrictions" on the basis that those restrictions harm both the former employees and the economy (a *public* interest) that is deprived of their services. In general, courts have frowned upon and invalidated blanket provisions that prevent a former employee from working for others in an industry longer than six or twelve months, primarily due to the financial impact on the employee, but also due to potential impacts on the public, which might lose the individual's economic contributions during the restriction period.

Unconscionability

Unconscionability is another concept courts use to re-write or nullify contracts, particularly where a party in a superior bargaining position has used that position to exact "unfair" terms. Notably, invalidation in a single case with a customer can invalidate the contract or offending provision as to all customers covered by the same contract or provision.

In 2016, for example, the Delaware Court of Chancery found that a defendant was improperly and unconscionably using an interest-only, non-amortizing installment loan to evade Delaware's Payday Loan Law.

And in a 2016 Michigan case, a plaintiff prevailed on an unconscionability claim to invalidate an account provision that permitted a bank to batch and reorder customers' transactions to maximize overdraft charges.

Unconscionability claims are very difficult to prove, particularly where consumers have other choices in the market, but win or lose, they usually create publicity headaches for corporate defendants.

As a preventative measure, any one-sided contract to be used in consumer transactions by an experienced dealer or provider should be reviewed by a competent lawyer.

The best way to forestall litigation and protect one-sided language from invalidation is to call it out in capitalized letters under an unambiguous caption and to include language explaining why the provision is appropriate and reasonable in the context.

The Parol Evidence Rule

A number of important contract law concepts are best explained and understood in relation to the *Parol Evidence Rule*. The Parol Evidence Rule is one of many rules of evidence that dictate what facts or other evidence can and cannot be introduced in a trial.

Even though not directly a rule of contracts, the *Parol Evidence Rule* impacts how contracts are interpreted and enforced by courts. The word "parol" comes from a Latin word meaning "oral."

The rule essentially says that, where a written contract is intended to be the parties' *entire agreement*, other evidence, either written or oral, cannot be introduced to say that the parties intended something else. The goal of the rule is to provide certainty in contractual relationships.

Exceptions to the Parol Evidence Rule

In a perfect world, all contracts would be drafted with precision and foresight, clearly and comprehensively describing the parties' intentions and accounting for the unexpected. Reality being what it is, not every contract meets this standard. As a result, courts have created a number of important exceptions to the prohibition against evidence "outside of the four corners" of a contract, i.e., not found within the contract language itself.

The following exceptions to the *Parol Evidence Rule* are often important in contract litigation. As with other concepts of contract law, understanding them in advance can aid in preventative drafting to avoid disputes down the road.

Ambiguity

Even where a contract recites that it contains the complete understanding of the parties and disclaims the existence of any other written or oral agreements or understandings, the *Parol Evidence Rule* will allow a party to introduce evidence outside of the contract to resolve an "ambiguity." An ambiguity is a term to which reasonable persons might assign different meanings — i.e. does "200 red pens" mean 200 pens with red ink or 200 pens with red exteriors? To the extent possible, contracts should be drafted to avoid ambiguities by assigning clear definitions to important terms, precisely describing the obligations of each party and carefully avoiding grammatical and word choice errors.

In practice, contracts are rarely free from all ambiguity, and, in any dispute, ambiguities are often among the first points of attack of any good lawyer.

Interpretation

Parol evidence may also be permitted by a court to "interpret" a contract in order to determine the parties' actual intent, but it will be permitted only to explain missing terms, not to contradict terms clearly provided for in the contract. The "Rules of Interpretation" discussion below goes into more detail on when and how courts decide whether parol evidence, also called "extrinsic" evidence, should be considered to better understand the parties' intent.

Mistake

Parol evidence can also be introduced to show the absence of mutual assent necessary for the creation of a contract in the first place. To qualify under the exception and to invalidate a contract, a mistake must be "held by both parties" – i.e., both parties were mistaken about a fact material to the formation of the contract.

A common example cited in text books is where party A agrees to pay party B a certain amount to drill a well to supply fresh water. After drilling at the place identified by A, B encounters impenetrable rock 20 feet down. Since both parties were mistaken about the feasibility of drilling the well, a court might nullify the contract on grounds of mistake.

A mistake in business judgment or mistake of fact by one party, however, will not nullify a contract. For example, if one party gets a great deal on a rare coin because the other party did not know its value, he or she cannot later seek to invalidate the transaction. That is *not* what is meant by the term mistake in contract law.

Awareness of a possible "mistake" issue during a negotiation might be a red flag warranting guidance from counsel.

Fraud, Duress

Like mistake, proof that a party entered into a contract under duress or in circumstances involving fraud by the other party is permitted as an exception to the *Parol Evidence Rule* in order to show the absence of voluntary mutual assent.

As one somewhat familiar example, a party stuck in a resort timeshare contract that has not turned out to be what the timeshare company represented might be able to invalidate the contract based on any documented fraudulent statements about things such as the likelihood of price appreciation, whether the timeshare contract was freely transferable, or even the degree to which the time share purchaser would enjoy booking priority over non–purchasing vacationers.

Similarly, an elderly person pressured into a timeshare contract following hours of high pressure sales tactics, including actions that made it difficult for the person to leave the sales presentation, might have a case for breaking the agreement due to claims of duress.

Promise versus Condition

Under older case law, each party's consideration in a contract takes the form of a promise(s) or condition(s). This distinction is less important under modern case law, but awareness of the issue helps to highlight the need for detailing the consequences of either party's potential performance failures.

Here are excerpted definitions of these terms from Black's Law Dictionary:

Promise: A declaration, verbal or written, made by one person to another for a good or valuable consideration in the nature of a covenant by which the promisor binds himself to do or forbear some act, and gives to the promisee a legal right to demand and enforce a fulfillment.

Condition: A future and uncertain event upon the happening of which is made to depend the existence of an obligation, or that which subordinates the existence of liability under a contract to a certain future event.

Failure by "party A" to perform on its promise(s) will always allow "party B" to seek damages from party A, but may or may not enable party B to withhold its performance.

Absent clear language, a court will try to ascertain the "*intent of the parties.*" This requires reading the contract as a whole and, if necessary, considering any evidence available to it under exceptions to the *Parol Evidence Rule*. The court may conclude that the promise not performed by party A does not excuse party B's performance, but merely creates a right in party B to pursue damages.

Under modern case law in most jurisdictions, however, if party A's breach is *material*, party B's performance will be excused and B would also likely be entitled to damages.

When a contract clearly states that party A's performance is a condition to party B's obligation to perform, then party B will be excused from performing if party A fails to perform.

This can create timing questions. What if party A performs, but only after the required time under the contract? Or what if party A performs, but not entirely, or perfectly? Courts sometimes view a right of termination as a drastic remedy and often look for something in the "intent of the parties" to support a less harsh outcome. Therefore, if party A's timely performance is indeed intended to be a condition to party B's performance, party B should insist on clear language to that effect, along with language specifically justifying that approach so a court knows it was both intended and negotiated. The following is an example of what that might look like:

> *"In the event Party A fails to provide the Delivery Truck in like-new condition by the Commencement Date, Party B shall be relieved of its obligations to provide the Delivery Services for Party A, as the parties acknowledge and agree that Party B has no cost-effective alternatives for providing the Delivery Services and also that Party B will need to promptly pursue other business opportunities in the event of such failure by Party A."*

Drafting performance obligations, remedies in the event of a party's breach, and rights and obligations in the event of contract termination are all discussed further in Chapter Two, *Common Mistakes,* Chapter Four, *Drafting,* and Chapter Five, *Common Contract Terms.*

Rules of Interpretation

Intent of the Parties

Most contract disputes involve questions of interpretation. Disputes can arise from different views of the same language or different ideas on how to deal with unanticipated gaps in the contract language. The goal of contract law is to *determine what the parties intended* at the time they entered into the agreement. This is done first and foremost by examining the contract language, and then, as necessary, the factual context.

With respect to unforeseen developments, courts must decide what result best reflects the intentions of the parties and produces an outcome that is *"reasonable."* In wrestling with such questions, courts have developed a number of *"rules of interpretation,"* sometimes also called *"rules of construction."* Knowing and applying the rules of interpretation in contract drafting can help reduce uncertainty.

Drafting to minimize issues of interpretation is often challenging for non-lawyers. This is because of the inherent subtleties of written language and the non-lawyer's inexperience in dealing with contract disputes, litigation, judges, juries and other aspects of law that are learned only by lawyering. With that caveat, here are some generally accepted rules of interpretation:

- **Plain Meaning.** Words are given their plain and normal meaning, except where the usage of a particular word has varied that meaning.

- **Technical Words.** Technical words, or words customary to a particular industry, will be given their technical or special meanings when used in that context.

- **Intentions of the Parties.** Words will be given the meaning that seems to best reflect the intentions of the parties.

- **Consistency with General Purposes.** Every part of a contract will be read in a manner that is consistent with its general purposes.

- **Surrounding Circumstances.** As described above under the *Parol Evidence Rule*, the circumstances surrounding a contract's negotiation may sometimes be shown to aid in its interpretation.

- **Narrow or Restricted Meanings.** Specific uses of a term or phrase in a contract may impose the same narrow or restricted meaning upon more general uses of the same term or phrase in a contract.

- **Lists.** Depending on the context and specific language used, detailed lists of similar items can be read to exclude items that are not similar. Conversely, a general list can be read to include more than those listed.

- **Reasonableness.** Where possible, a contract will be interpreted to render it reasonable rather than unreasonable.

- **Non-Drafting Party Bias.** Given competing meanings, a court will generally favor the one urged by the non-drafting party.

Courts use these rules to standardize how language will be interpreted in the event of a dispute. The goal is always to determine and give effect to the *"intent of the parties."*

First and foremost then, parties to an agreement should attempt to summarize their intentions. As discussed below in Chapter Five, *Common Contract Terms*, the intent of the parties can be explained in the "recitals" or "whereas" clauses at the top of the agreement.

Other drafting tips for clarifying the intent of the parties:

- Avoid words, clauses, or sentences that may have more than one meaning. This includes being sensitive to the different outcomes that the use of "and" can have when "or" is the better choice and visa versa.

- Place adverbs, adjectives, and other modifiers with precision and use appropriate grammatical techniques and punctuation to achieve clarity.

- Lastly, use terms consistently. Contract drafting is not the same as creative writing — avoid using a variety of terms to express the same meanings. Contracts need to be clear, not interesting.

Implied Covenant of Good Faith and Fair Dealing

As noted above under *Rules of Interpretation*, between two competing interpretations of a contract provision, courts will often favor the one that renders the provision reasonable rather than unreasonable.

Similarly, courts in many jurisdictions in the United States recognize *an implied covenant of good faith and fair dealing* in contractual relationships. This implied covenant generally requires the parties to act honestly and fairly with each other. Fraudulent, evasive, oppressive, dishonest or otherwise unfair conduct by one party against another has been deemed to violate the covenant.

The implied covenant of good faith is in tension, though, with two fundamental tenets of contract law: (1) the freedom of parties to contract as they wish, and (2) the right of each party to act in its own best commercial interest. As a result, while commonly followed in some form or another in most states, it is not recognized in every country, including England, for example.

As discussed in more detail in Chapter 8, *Dispute Resolution*, a party that can point to violations of specific contractual provisions supported by provable facts usually has the upper hand in a dispute. Barring such facts, however, if one party to an agreement has acted in a morally reprehensible manner that prevented the other party from receiving "the fruits of its bargain" or that "frustrates the overarching purpose of the agreement," some states, like California, may allow a claim and damages based on a breach of the implied covenant of good faith.

Here are some examples where the covenant might be successfully invoked:

- Intentionally withholding critical information from the other party.

- Intentionally performing poorly in order to extract concessions from the other party, particularly if done by a party in a much more powerful position.

- Failing to provide reasonable cooperation necessary for the other party's performance or otherwise interfering with or thwarting the other party's performance.

- Seeking to terminate an agreement based on false or highly exaggerated claims of breach by the other party.

- Willful conduct intended to cause commercial harm to the other party.

In particularly egregious cases involving fraud or extremely harmful conduct, some jurisdictions might even allow for punitive damages and attorneys' fees in a "bad faith" case. But such awards are highly disfavored under contract law except in the unique area of insurance contracts and should not be a primary factor in deciding whether or not to litigate.

Tort Claims

As discussed in Chapter Eight, *Dispute Resolution,* punitive damages and attorneys' fees, generally disallowed under contract law, can be awarded in "tort" claims – i.e., wrongful conduct that causes harm to others. Torts alleged in business include, among others, fraud, tortious interference with a contract, and theft of trade secrets.

While courts often reject attempts to convert negligent contract performance claims into tort claims, or to combine the two, courts have accepted tort claims in contracts cases where there are clear injuries from breaches of any duties that *arise independently from the contract terms.*

It is somewhat common, for example, to see both breach of contract claims and the tort claim "fraud in the inducement," or simply "fraudulent inducement," in the same lawsuit. In such cases, the plaintiff is arguing both that the defendant breached the terms of the parties' agreement, but also that the parties' agreement should be entirely invalidated because the defendant induced the plaintiff to enter into the agreement by means of fraudulent statements.

Additionally, tort claims alleging *professional negligence* against professional service providers are also often permitted in addition to or instead of contract claims against the same professional service provider.

Waiver, Modification

Waiver and *Modification* are two different but logically related concepts that both involve intentional or unintentional changes to the obligations of one or both parties to an agreement. Sometimes a party will ask the other party for a waiver or modification during the course of performance as a result of a change in intentions or circumstances. Other times, once a dispute has arisen, issues of waiver or modification are raised as defenses to non-performance. Both highlight the need to avoid casually undermining or clouding the parties' original obligations to one another.

Waiver

Sometimes a party's performance will vary from or fall short of what is required under a contract. If the other party expressly accepts the lesser performance without complaining, despite having time and opportunity to do so, that party may later be deemed to have "waived" its ability under the contract to complain and seek full performance, a refund, or damages.

As an example, if party A has long accepted party B's delivery of inventory items on the 15th of each month without complaint despite the contract's requirement that delivery occur on the 1st of each month, a court might reject party A's sudden claim of breach, based on party B's argument that Party A "waived" the requirement of timely delivery. We'll discuss drafting to avoid waiver issues in Chapter Five under *"Modification and Waiver."*

Modification

The concept of modification is similar to waiver in that parties to a contract may later agree to changes, either orally or in writing. Any modification, often captioned in writing as an "Amendment" or "Addendum," should be handled with the same care as the original contract. When handled by non-lawyers, modifications are often made orally or by other informal means. In larger organizations, employees should be cautioned to avoid saying or doing things without proper authorization that could be interpreted by others outside of the organization as modifying important contractual requirements negotiated by others in the organization.

Waiver and modification issues can result in costly "he-said, she-said" battles. This is an area of contract law where dispute avoidance requires attention during both contract drafting and implementation.

Drafting considerations are discussed in Chapter Five under *"Modification and Waiver."* Chapter Six, *"Implementation,"* describes techniques for monitoring both parties' performance of contract obligations and for communicating issues or concerns that might arise as to either party's performance, changed circumstances, or other matters.

Letters of Intent and Oral Contracts

These two subjects are addressed together because mistakes in either area tend to open a Pandora's Box of issues regarding contract formation and enforceability, intent of the parties, parol evidence, and remedies, just to name a few.

Letters of Intent

"Letters of Intent," or *"LOIs,"* are often used by parties during an exploratory phase of discussions. They express mutual intentions to move forward toward a contractual arrangement, but are, by their terms, non-binding. Here is a typical LOI introductory paragraph:

> *This letter of intent is for discussion purposes only and sets forth certain principal terms of a proposed commercial agreement between Gadget Manufacturing, Inc. and Gadget Sensor Supplier, Inc. This letter of intent is not intended to be a binding agreement between the parties regarding the subject matter hereof. A binding agreement will not occur unless and until the parties have agreed upon the terms of the transaction and such terms are included in the appropriate definitive agreement that has been negotiated, approved, executed and delivered by each party hereto.*

When done correctly, an LOI describes a mutual undertaking the parties are considering and further states that, in the event the parties are unable to negotiate an acceptable written contract, neither party is bound to take any further action. An LOI should include nothing that contradicts this except that each party might explicitly agree to protect and not misuse the other party's confidential information and one party might even agree to pay the other's pre-approved expenses.

Negotiating an LOI gives the parties an opportunity to sketch out a rough term sheet and provides each party with a document that can be shared with others in the organization, such as a Board of Directors, who need to understand what is being negotiated and why.

Misuse of LOIs

Often, unfortunately, once parties start writing an LOI, they get carried away and try to accomplish too much in it, describing the terms of a relationship in too much detail and often providing for one or both parties to begin performance while negotiations continue on a final agreement.

The misuse of LOIs can be a problem in organizations lacking policy and procedural checks and balances to regulate the impatience or naiveté of individual team members. Be quietly alert for the possibility that talk of an LOI is a red flag for a potentially troubled commercial relationship. Variations on the following pattern sometimes play out around LOIs, especially in startups:

- An LOI is used as a morale booster to portray a deal as all-but-certain;
- Whether or not spelled out in the LOI, work begins on some aspect(s) of the project;
- Signing of the LOI distracts attention from timely finalizing a real agreement;
- Work on the project evolves beyond the LOI's terms and problems are encountered; and
- One of the parties decides to terminate the project and disappointments and uncertainties abound.

However one gets there, reliance on an LOI to begin work, combined with the parties' later communications, acts of performance, and other "course of conduct," can set the stage for claims of damages, lost opportunities, compromised intellectual property, wasted resources, and other counterproductive outcomes.

When LOIs Create Enforceable Obligations

What laypersons often do not understand is that an LOI's talismanic language stating that no agreement exists until there is a final agreement can be subverted. As in nature, the law exists in part to fill vacuums it deems unfair. Legal theories such as *"detrimental reliance," "oral contract," "unjust enrichment"* and *"quantum meruit"* (Latin for "as much as deserved") can and will be summoned where economically feasible to right perceived wrongs, or even to take advantage of the weaker or less sophisticated of the two parties.

LOI Best Practices

Because of the tendency to misunderstand and misuse LOIs, they should be discouraged if those managing the process are inexperienced. Where business dynamics make avoidance of an LOI impossible, the following conditions should be observed:

- LOIs should be drafted narrowly and precisely, with the help of a lawyer if possible.

- Performance by either party should be forbidden except when absolutely critical, and then only within very limited and explicitly described boundaries and with costs clearly allocated.

- Any LOI should be quickly followed by a comprehensive agreement that the parties can sign as soon as they have decided to go forward.

Oral Agreements

Somewhat akin to LOIs, oral agreements between parties that are performable within a year and not for the purchase of real estate are generally valid and enforceable.

Despite their technical validity, it is best to avoid oral agreements. First, they are subject to obvious problems of proof. In the event of any type of dispute, how will the injured party present his or her case?

Further, even the most casual arrangements can pose hidden or unforeseeable risks of non-performance, inflated charges, and a range of potentially serious liabilities.

For example, should the vendor that provides your office with coffee or bottled water do so without an agreement? What if one of the vendor's employees hurts himself with his own equipment on your property? What if the vendor's employee harasses or injures one of your employees or customers? A written document could compel the vendor to carry insurance and indemnify your company from all such losses and expenses – remedies a court might not award absent a written agreement.

Similarly, a simple agreement with a company to provide cleaning services for your offices can and should include indemnification provisions as well as specific warranties and representations around licenses, worker background checks, insurance, and protection of confidential information.

In summary, it is difficult to draw a line of materiality or significance below which oral agreements make sense, particularly since most responsible business persons have some form of standard agreement to offer as a starting point. In fact, resistance by any business person to a signed, written agreement should be a red flag prompting questions about insurance certificates, appropriate bonds or licenses, tax ID numbers, and other documentation.

Breach, Damages and Remedies

Breach

Under contract law, a party can breach contractual obligations accidentally, intentionally, or even through no fault of its own due to circumstances beyond its control.

In this respect, breach of contract is somewhat similar to the concept of "strict liability" in tort law concerning dangerously defective goods. Under strict liability, if a baby stroller design includes a hidden defect that pinches off babies' fingers, liability cannot be avoided simply because the design defect was accidental or even difficult to have avoided. Similarly, a contract breach is a breach, regardless of intent or level of diligence.

And while showing "negligence," a tort law concept, is not required to prove a breach of non-performance, negligence in performing contractual obligations can *sometimes* constitute its own breach for which damages are owed, particularly where professional or technical services are involved and a certain *duty of care and level of skill customary within the profession* is required to properly perform the services.

As discussed further in Chapter 5, *Common Contract Terms*, most contracts do not have a section captioned "*Breach,*" let alone a section captioned *"Remedies."* This might be because many think the subject of possible performance failings is too negative to dwell on.

As a result, analyzing questions of breach and remedies after the fact is often an uncertain exercise. It usually involves harmonizing often-deficient *Obligations* and *Termination* language with conflicting provisions under *Disclaimers of Warranties* and *Limitations of Liability,* as will be discussed in later chapters.

Damages

In contract law, *damages* is the legal term for dollar amounts one owes in order to put the non-breaching party in the same economic position as if no breach had occurred. Unless specifically disclaimed or limited by contractual language, this generally means both losses sustained and gains prevented, minus losses or missed opportunities that could have been reasonably avoided or mitigated.

"Losses sustained" in this calculation could include things like expenses incurred by the non-breaching party to replace the product or service not timely or properly provided. They could also mean expenses incurred in reliance on and in preparation for the breaching party's performance, including collateral expenses such as advertising the product or service that was dependent upon the breaching party's performance.

"Gains prevented" could theoretically include lost profits, lost increases in company value, and the value of other missed opportunities caused by the breach.

In calculating losses sustained, courts have looked at whether expenses incurred by a non-breaching party were reasonable and whether or not they could have been "salvaged" for the same or another purpose. Similarly, damages for "gains prevented" can be reduced by evidence of lack of "certainty" and by evidence that such damages were (or could have been) avoided or reduced through substitutions or other available efforts to reduce the damages, often referred to as *"mitigation."*

The potential for relatively open-ended damages under the case law is the reason that virtually all commercial agreements include *Limitations of Liability* clauses specifically disclaiming liability for indirect losses such as lost profits. *Limitations of Liability* clauses are discussed further in Chapter Five, *Common Contract Terms.*

Remedies

Remedies is a broader term than damages. It covers a wide range of rights and obligations that can arise when a party breaches its contractual obligations, including claims for damages. Potential remedies can include, among other things:

- rights to compel performance or to provide substituted performance,

- rights to terminate for cause,

- rights to fee or price reductions or refunds,

- rights to compensation for direct or indirect damages, and

- rights to "indemnification" for losses and expenses related to third party claims.

An interesting tenet of contract law is that, except as limited in writing, the damages to which a party will be entitled for another party's breach are fairly broad and need not be detailed in an agreement. This may be one of the most important things to know about how contract case law has evolved – contract law may be a form of private law created between two parties, but it has teeth.

A related point is the general rule that all potential remedies - contractual, common law, statutory, or equitable - are "cumulative," meaning that several different types of damages and other remedies can be awarded for the same facts.

If a parts supplier delivers defective parts to an auto manufacturer, and the manufacturer incorporates those parts into its vehicles before discovering the defects, the manufacturer could have multiple (cumulative) damage claims against the supplier, to the extent not limited under their agreement, including: (i) refunds of amounts paid for the parts, (ii) all costs associated with recalling and fixing the vehicles with replacement parts, (iii) costs and expenses relating to any customer lawsuits or regulatory actions stemming from the defective parts, and (iv) any lost profits suffered by the manufacturer that can be attributed to the resulting bad publicity.

This rule applies *absent* a specific contractual provision, or absent a strong suggestion from the contract language, that one or more remedies provided in a contract are "exclusive."

Silence on Remedies as a Drafting Strategy

The above two points mean that silence on remedies can be a valid drafting tactic *if* an agreement does not already contain unduly restrictive *Disclaimers of Warranties* and *Limitations of Liabilities.* These concepts will be discussed further in Chapter Five, *Common Contract Terms.*

Silence, instead of spelling out specific remedies, might be the better strategy, for example, if the other party is known to be strongly averse to incorporating remedies or if the other party might respond with potentially severe *Disclaimers of Warranty* and *Limitations of Liability* provisions that would limit potential damages worse than mere silence on remedies.

In Chapter Two, *Common Mistakes,* we'll discuss the challenges of incorporating meaningful remedies in agreements and the potential benefits of persevering to do so.

Risk that Remedies Language May be Deemed Exclusive

Another point worth considering is the possibility that poorly drafted *Remedies* clauses might provide a non-breaching party less than what might have been available under the law, particularly if those stated remedies are later cast, fairly or unfairly, as "exclusive" remedies under the agreement. As an example, a *Remedies* clause specifically providing for rights to (i) terminate for cause and (ii) receive a refund of all fees paid, could be viewed restrictively by a court as being the exclusive remedies for breach, as negotiated by the parties.

Addressing this concern is relatively easy, assuming the other party goes along. Whenever remedies provisions are included in an agreement, the buyer should also add language to the effect that "the remedies described here are in addition to all other appropriate remedies under the Agreement or under law."

Benefits of Strong Remedies Language

Despite such drafting risks and despite the default rule that damages are available to a non-breaching party, whether or not specifically provided for, the better approach in most cases is to think through the types of breaches the seller might commit, negotiate for the best possible remedies, and incorporate them into the agreement.

One of the most compelling reasons for doing so is the fact that litigating to enforce rights under almost any agreement is very expensive, time consuming, stressful, and often quite uncertain. Parties that have written provisions detailing performance obligations and meaningful remedies for breach are far less likely to have unexpected disagreements. Among other reasons for this, greater clarity on the costs of breach reduces the danger that a party will breach intentionally based on a miscalculation of the costs and benefits.

Additionally, in the event of a dispute, clarity in an agreement around performance obligations and remedies for breach will put the non-breaching party in a much better position to make its case to a court or arbitrator. A stronger case can mean reduced costs, fees and uncertainty, and potentially even a faster path to victory in the form of an earlier settlement or even a successful "Motion for Summary Judgement."

Summary of Contract Law

This chapter started by noting that contracts create private law. When a contract is validly entered into, this private law can be publicly enforced through litigation. At the dispute stage, contract law is devoted largely to determining and effectuating, as best possible, the "intent of the parties."

The overarching lessons from this chapter can be distilled to five points: (i) know the elements required for, or that can trigger, an enforceable contract, (ii) always draft contracts that are clear, accurate, and sufficiently comprehensive so that principles of contract law are *not called upon* to fill gaps, correct errors, and make sense of ambiguities, (iii) describe performance obligations in the greatest detail possible, (iv) where possible, include comprehensive remedies to prevent or mitigate potential disputes, and (v) keep in mind the implied covenant of good faith and fair dealing.

These concepts of Contract Law, in turn, all reinforce a key theme of this book, i.e., that contract disputes are costly and distracting and avoiding them should be a priority for any business person.

Spelling out rights, obligations, expectations, and remedies as clearly as possible minimizes risks associated with possible disputes by (i) weeding out unqualified or otherwise questionable commercial partners, (ii) encouraging better performance from those who might otherwise be tempted to cut corners, (iii) increasing the likelihood that a breaching party will reach a reasonable resolution short of litigation, and (iv) increasing the likelihood of a faster, better outcome in the event of litigation, arbitration, or other dispute resolution processes.

Chapter Two

COMMON MISTAKES

While understanding contract law is certainly helpful in drafting and negotiating contracts, the most common and costly mistakes tend to involve simple errors in due diligence, judgment and drafting, and giving up too easily on important issues. The following mistakes are common sources of commercial disputes. Avoid them to prevent costly litigation, missed opportunities and wasted resources.

Performance before Agreement

Whether based on mutually euphoric *"good faith"* or naive reliance on an LOI, one of the worst mistakes is having one or both parties begin performance before a final agreement is in place. Those who do this often see themselves as entrepreneurial risk takers. The predictably bad outcomes often make such decisions seem impulsive and undisciplined in hindsight.

Here are some of the justifications you might use yourself or hear from others when pre-agreement performance is happening or being considered:

> *"The parties trust each other enough to move forward in good faith; the contract will come together in due time."*

"We'll keep working on the contract, but the work has to start now to meet the project deadline."

"The other party is a business partner, not a vendor. I'm not worried about the contract."

"Concern over the contract will show lack of trust and jeopardize the relationship."

"An LOI will give us an opportunity to see how the other party performs before we sign."

"We'll get a better deal once the other side feels committed."

Starting performance prior to having an agreement often takes organizations backward from where they started, or at least sideways. This is because, by the time the mistake is realized, the organization may have to first dig out of a mess before it can start over.

Walking away from a failed relationship might involve more than just walking away from already incurred sunken costs and critically delayed opportunities - the other party may also have valid claims for additional compensation. Additionally, rights to any jointly created intellectual property may need to be sorted out between the parties, through amicable means or otherwise.

Managing Impatience

Impatience is the most common factor in proceeding without a final agreement. The decision to charge ahead before an agreement is in place often comes under tight deadlines, and sometimes when a difficult issue or two remain unresolved after two or more turns of a draft agreement.

Eventually, though, these very issues may bring about the relationship's undoing. Putting off difficult issues does not make them easier to resolve. Often, in fact, the opposite will be true. Once the relationship has started, the other party may have less incentive to compromise, particularly if you have already written checks or performed your part.

Prevent impatience from impacting contract negotiations in the first place by accepting and embracing the fact that it is quite common for sophisticated parties to exchange multiple drafts of important documents as they reach compromises and narrow their differences.

Failing to Shop and Compare

RFPs

Depending on the size, importance and complexity of an expected relationship, it is generally wise to look at more than one option before entering into serious negotiations. At the conservative end of the spectrum, significant relationships are often preceded by a *"Request for Proposals"* or *"RFP."* This is a document sent to prospective providers of a needed good or service that describes in detail the requested good or service, specifying exactly how interested parties are to respond and by when.

Multiple Bids

If a full RFP is too burdensome, it is still wise to follow the traditional rule of *getting two or three bids* for any commercial procurement of goods or services. At a minimum, going through either process will help an organization assess its objectives and expectations and prepare it for incorporating those in a final agreement.

RFP Follow-up

Answers to RFPs are often carefully written. They should be carefully studied and follow-up information should be requested where answers seem incomplete, evasive or otherwise miss the mark. Depending on the nature of the proposed arrangement and your level of certainty or uncertainty about the abilities, facilities, and reputation of the parties involved, you may want to perform additional due diligence by visiting and inspecting facilities, talking with customer and creditor references, and pulling reports on financial condition, judgments and the like.

Incorporate RFP into Final Agreement

Lastly, consider adding a party's finalized RFP response as an exhibit to any agreement entered into with them, along with language in the agreement making the RFP response part of the agreement.

Fallback Options

An added benefit of scrutinizing and engaging with more than one prospect is that, if contract negotiations do not go well, you may have a viable fallback option. Even if you do not resort to that option, the knowledge that you have an option will make you a better negotiator.

Inadequate Descriptions of Performance Obligations

Detailed Performance Obligations

Performance shortcomings are surprisingly common in business. Sellers of goods and services can disappoint for any number of reasons, including over-promising, corner-cutting, staffing problems, phasing out a product line or service, selling a product line or service to another company, and simple incompetence or lack of diligence.

As a result, performance concerns are possibly the top source of commercial disputes. As discussed in Chapter Five under *"Obligations of the Parties,"* every contract should clearly and completely describe each party's performance obligations.

These descriptions should include all of the details that the parties have discussed, and particularly all of the representations the other party has made, either directly or indirectly through representations of their staff members or through their advertising or marketing materials.

As noted above, if the other party provided a written RFP response, consider attaching it to the agreement if it contains the best description of the other party's obligations and possibly also specific representations and warranties.

Get it in Writing

It is much easier to make another party perform as you expect if those expectations have been clearly written into the contract. In the end, it does not matter what the sales or "business development" person told you if it is not in the agreement. As discussed in Chapter Five, *Common Contract Terms*, most contracts contain a clause captioned along the lines of *Entire Agreement* that specifically disclaims the enforceability of any written or oral promises or representations made but not incorporated into the agreement.

In the face of resistance to detailing performance obligations, sometimes it helps to tell the sales person or other negotiator that, while you *believe and trust them*, others in their organization and in your organization will also be required to understand and administer the agreement in the future, so the details need to be in writing.

Aversion to Detail is a Red Flag

Another party's refusal to add detailed performance obligations to an agreement is always a red flag. Take it as a clue that the other party does not intend to perform as you are hoping or expecting. Rarely does a party's performance exceed their written commitments. Many get burned by assuming others will perform at a high level for reputational reasons. Reputational concerns, unfortunately, are not always the driving force one would expect.

Bad Outcomes

The mistake of failing to detail performance obligations causes some of the worst contractual nightmares. If proper performance is not clearly defined, poor performance likely will not constitute a breach of the agreement, making remedies such as offsets, price reductions or termination unavailable. Paying full price for the wrong product or service is a bad outcome. If the agreement is for an extended term, the only recourse may be to negotiate a large termination fee just so you can walk away and pay a new provider all over.

Rough Learning Experience

A client of the author once signed just such an agreement relating to a backend technology conversion against the author's strongly worded advice and ultimately paid a $1.5 million fee for absolutely nothing but a rough learning experience. The contract in question contained few representations about what the technology platform could do. Soon after signing, the client realized that the platform could not do what was needed. In addition to the negotiated $1.5 million termination fee, the company's mistake wasted substantial internal resources, delayed a number of important projects tied to the system conversion, and severely harmed staff morale.

Weak or Nonexistent Remedies

As noted above, poorly drafted performance obligations are possibly the top source of commercial disputes; weak or non-existent remedies could be a close second.

Unlike some areas of contract negotiation, *Remedies* is a difficult topic to reduce to simple, actionable pearls of wisdom. As noted above, there are many types of remedies; there are also an infinite number of ways to draft them, disclaim them, and limit them. And while the law generously provides for all kinds of damages for contract breaches, the almost universal tendency of sellers is to vigorously resist detailed remedies provisions and to disclaim and limit liabilities.

The typical seller negotiating position is essentially, "Why should we agree to damages that could greatly exceed the value of the agreement?" Such sellers are often unmoved by typical buyers' responses such as, "If the losses were foreseeable and you caused them, why not?" Well-coached sellers often come back with comments like, "We simply cannot agree to unknown and potentially ruinous liabilities; we cannot be your insurer." As discussed in Chapter Five regarding *Insurance* clauses, the correct response to this type of rebuttal is often "Maybe not, but your insurer can and should be our insurer for any liabilities caused by your performance."

Benefits of Detailed Remedies

Despite these negotiating and drafting challenges, it is a mistake to give up too quickly. Pushing sellers for the right remedies is worth the effort and the inevitable friction.

Even though the law theoretically provides damages for breach whether specifically agreed to or not, contractual breach remedies can make the difference between success or failure in a commercial relationship. Contracts with clear and meaningful remedies provide (i) incentives for better performance, (ii) leverage for forcing faster performance corrections, and (iii) greater certainty regarding the outcome of potential litigation or other dispute resolution processes, all of which reduce the likelihood of disputes in the first place.

Chipping Away at Resistance to Remedies

In almost any commercial negotiating context, simply expect to take heat for bringing up potential performance issues and related remedies, and be prepared to persevere thoughtfully and creatively to get the best deal you can.

In many cases, the only viable strategy is a back-and-forth process of proposing and explaining appropriate remedies, responding to rejections with alternate formulations of remedies, and simultaneously pushing back on and whittling away at any caps, disclaimers, and limitations that would unfairly limit the proposed remedies.

These strategies will be discussed further in Chapter Five, *Common Contract Terms*, including how to raise possible insurance solutions to help move remedies, disclaimers and limitations discussions in a positive direction.

The Importance of Backup Plans

While this back-and-forth process may eventually break a seller's will to resist fair remedies, sometimes it does not. The buyer must then make a difficult business judgment based on imperfect information about the potential value of a relationship and its potential risks.

In such cases, having a backup plan in the form of an alternative provider or approach can be invaluable. And as we have all learned when buying a car, sometimes the only way to get what you want is to walk away.

Strategies for overcoming these types of objections are discussed in Chapter Five under *Remedies for Breach*. Ultimately, the best guidance is simply to try to get the best remedies possible under the circumstances, whether with your first choice provider or with a backup alternative.

Poor Vetting of Vendors, Suppliers and Others

Selecting companies and persons to do business with requires good judgment. A tightly drafted contract does not provide absolute protection from business, legal, financial, regulatory, or third-party liability risk. Contractual protections from such risks usually depend on the strength and solvency of the other party and, less frequently, any available insurance.

Consequently, success in forming business relationships requires great care. Be on guard to identify and avoid con artists, blustering sales persons, and others who may mean well, but who simply lack the integrity or intellectual capacity to avoid making promises they cannot honor.

Clues

Whatever the titles of the individual or individuals with whom you are dealing – CEO, founder, head of business development - there are certain signs of trouble that should not be ignored. Too slick or too friendly? Disinterested in details? Pressure to sign quickly and/or pay up front? Unwilling to put promises made orally in writing? Trust your eyes, your ears, your brain, and your gut.

Eject!

If you find yourself in a relationship with a con artist or over-promising incompetent, promptly exercise any and all available remedies and rights of termination under your contract. Do not get further duped or guilted into "working through the problems." Doing so could limit or eliminate what remedies remain by creating issues of waiver, modification, detrimental reliance or "quantum meruit."

Blindly Accepting "Standard Contracts"

Unless you are looking at a "click-wrap" software agreement or the standard terms and conditions for a credit card, always assume that you can propose edits! When necessary, insist on doing so. Unfortunately too many non-lawyers give up very easily in the face of resistance over making changes to "form" or "standard" agreements.

Reputable companies that are serious about providing value and growing their businesses often have acceptable standard agreements. You might need to strike the clause subjecting you to the courts of Cedar Rapids and boost the remedies section a bit, but that may be all. Other times, substantial revisions are required. You may need to get past the other party's insistence that the standard agreement is not negotiable.

Appealing to the other party's fairness or sense of reason works most of the time. Credibly threatening to walk from the deal should work in just about every other situation. In any event, you should read the contract. If it is unacceptable or incomprehensible, insist on changes or find a new provider of the particular product or service.

Just do not just fall for the line that a template cannot be modified. Sellers usually want your business enough to change a few words here and there, even if it means they have to consult with their internal or external lawyers.

Duration Too Long or Too Short

Do not make the mistake of accepting the first "term" or "termination date" drafted into an agreement dictating its duration.

Contracts can often be for as long or as short as you need them to be. If you have doubts about a person or company, set up an agreement as a 90 day test with an option to extend. If you need to lock in a critical supplier for several years, do so.

But keep in mind the increasing pace of change when signing contracts for longer than one year, particularly contracts that involve technologies, goods or services that may soon be obsolete or a lot cheaper.

One year contracts that renew annually if neither party opts out with proper notice work well for many types of relationships, provided it is okay if both parties have the ability to terminate each year rather than renew. Always make sure processes and systems are in place to allow for timely evaluation of contracts with upcoming automatic renewal notice deadlines, as further discussed in Chapter Six, *Implementation.*

Term and termination concepts are discussed again in greater detail in Chapter Six, *Common Contract Terms.*

Poor Document Change Tracking and Proofing

A negotiator must keep track of what is agreed to in negotiations and the responsive changes that have been made in the draft document. When the other side sends a new "mark-up" of an agreement, always carefully check their revisions against what has been agreed to. Sometimes revised documents resemble the discussions and sometimes they do not.

Problems can often be attributed simply to bad drafting – not everyone is equally talented at capturing oral points of agreement in clear, accurate text. But if you sign a document and later find out it does not say what you thought it said, you are out of luck. Although some courts might refuse to enforce changes furtively slipped into a document by the other side at the last minute, obtaining such vindication through the courts is uncertain and costly. Diligence in "turning drafts" is discussed further in Chapter Four, *Drafting.*

Chapter Three

NEGOTIATION

Negotiation Training

Although careful drafting is important, key ground is often won or lost in discussions before and during drafting. The same skills used by poker players and savvy car buyers also work well in business negotiations. Almost anyone can learn the basics of effective negotiation.

A great way for anyone to improve their negotiating skills is to attend a reputable negotiation strategy seminar. These tend to focus on:

- how to plan and prepare for negotiations by deciding what you want to achieve, knowing your priorities, and knowing your alternatives, particularly your "BATNA," or "best alternative to a negotiated agreement;

- how to assess the other party's position – their strengths, weaknesses, priorities and alternatives;

- how to test and validate your assumptions about the other party's position;

- how to frame the other party's perception of issues in order to find areas for compromise; and

- how to identify issues where both parties can trade off.

If you negotiate on a team of two or more, try to make sure less experienced team members receive training also, since success or failure is often determined by a negotiating team's weakest link. Once your less skilled colleague reveals your lack of viable alternatives, the importance of specific issues, your real or imagined timing constraints, or other weaknesses in your position, it is very difficult to re-set the talks. The other side naturally becomes more aggressive and inflexible. Good negotiation training can prevent rookie mistakes from ruining deals and careers.

Demeanor and Attitude

Just like in poker and car buying, your demeanor, character and attitude all impact contract negotiations. In every negotiation, you should be professional, courteous and reasonable. In most cases, you will get more of what you want if the other party likes and respects you. It is often not helpful, however, to be overly chatty in trying to win the friendship of the other side. Whether they realize it or not, chatty negotiators come across as weak and often provide important clues to the other side. It is best to watch what you say without seeming aloof or arrogant.

Body Language

Continuing the poker analogy, negotiate in a consistently thoughtful, emotionally neutral, and confident manner to avoid tipping your hand on issues of importance or weaknesses in your position.

Approach every negotiation with a positive attitude, but with the mindset that you can walk away if necessary. This almost always results in a better business deal than being emotionally predisposed to getting a deal at all cost. The more eager or desperate party almost always ends up conceding more and getting less than the party willing to "think about" the issues for a day or two.

Whether we realize it or not, how we feel is often telegraphed to the other side through our expressions, words and body language. Fidgeting, hand-clasping, leg bouncing, heel or toe tapping and face touching all signal nervousness that the other side can use to its advantage. To project confidence and trustworthiness, relax, smile, maintain eye contact, keep your feet planted on the ground, keep your hands relatively still, lean in a bit, maintain an open posture, and speak in a pleasant, non-confrontational manner.

Get the Other Side Talking

The most productive way to avoid chatting too much to your own detriment in a negotiation is to get the other side talking and listen attentively. As we know, people love to talk about themselves and what is important to them. The more you let someone talk in a negotiation, the more they will probably like you and trust you, and the more you will learn about negotiating with them.

Prepare by researching the other side and thinking about your questions to them in advance. The following are examples of good, open-ended questions to get another party talking in a negotiation:

- What is important to your team in these discussions?

- What would be a good outcome for you?

- Are there specific reasons that you are interested in working with our company?

- Do you have any specific concerns we should know about?

- Are there issues or opportunities outside of what we've discussed that would be helpful for us to learn more about?

Listen for:

- Clues about what the other side might be willing to trade off.

- Issues they might stick on.

- Carrots you can throw into the deal to get more of what you want.

Be prepared for the possibility that the other side is less concerned about the details of the specific deal in front of you and more focused on getting additional or different business from you down the road, or even just referrals to others for similar business. Assume nothing. You will almost always learn more from listening carefully than from talking too much about your own concerns or views.

Negotiating Chips

It is usually helpful to raise at least one or two issues or concerns that are secretly of lower importance than others. These can be thought of as negotiating chips to be given up strategically if necessary, while holding firm on issues of greater importance. Do not risk your credibility by lying about how important these peripheral issues might be, but touch on them and keep them on the list until it is useful to trade them for other concessions.

If, for example, timing of performance is less important to you than price, hold the line on price but eventually offer some timing flexibility if that is important to the other side. Another example discussed below in Chapter Five, *Common Contract*

Terms, is insurance – i.e., starting out with more rigorous insurance requirements for the other party than you might ultimately be willing to accept.

Do Not Negotiate Against Yourself

"Negotiating against yourself" involves offering concessions in exchange for nothing. It is the opposite of effective negotiation, and it can take on several forms and occur at different points in a negotiation.

Perhaps most commonly it involves offering a price for your goods or services and then offering a lower price before a counter offer has been received. Another common example involves over-anticipating the other party's concerns or positions and offering concessions before they are requested.

Interestingly, those prone to this negotiating error often do so later in talks after winning key points by throwing in unnecessary and unrequested concessions, usually with some vague expectation of increased good will.

Once terms have been agreed upon, the best approach is simply to say something like – "This all sounds good. We will incorporate the points we have agreed upon and circulate another draft of the agreement."

Negotiation Psychology

Despite the best of intentions, offering additional concessions after terms have been agreed upon often causes an adverse psychological reaction, making the other party suspect they negotiated a bad deal, not unlike receiving holiday gifts from vendors and service providers that seem excessively lavish.

Interestingly, newer leaders often commit this mistake, but so do more experienced sales and business development professionals. New leaders sometimes simply want to demonstrate their authority. In other cases, individuals negotiate against their interests or their company's interests in order to be liked by the other side, or because they are nervous or under too much pressure, or simply because they are too excited to stop talking.

In summary, a pattern of negotiating against oneself may be a sign that the guilty party lacks the nerves, confidence, or discipline to be a good negotiator. Any good negotiation training course will take these and others issues head-on through workshop exercises to uncover personal strengths and weaknesses and to offer strategies for making the most of one's mix of skills and personality traits.

Conflicts of Interests

Some companies and other organizations set themselves up for bad deals by having persons with financial incentives that are tied to signing "deals" negotiate those deals on their own. It is great to be on the other side of such situations, like when a business development person needs to meet a year-end quota or bonus goal. The conflicted sales person will concede almost any point you raise. When a member of your own team tips their hand about needing the deal, it is hard to undo the damage.

Because of this common compensation dynamic, it usually makes business sense to negotiate important agreements in "good cop – bad cop" teams – i.e., the friendly "let's get the deal done" business person and a manager, controller, CFO, or in-house counsel who takes the blame for sticking on important financial or technical issues. Once the deal is done, the friendlier negotiators can take the lead in mending fences if necessary.

Protection of Confidential Information

Before any negotiation or pre-negotiation discussions begin, you must decide whether or not to require the other party to sign a "non-disclosure agreement," or "NDA," to protect trade secrets, business opportunities, and other confidential information from improper use or sharing with third parties. In reviewing or drafting an NDA, it is important to confirm several key points:

- The description of what constitutes "Confidential Information" is broad enough and specific enough to protect what is important.

- The duration of the protection is sufficiently long, particularly for trade secrets.

- The exceptions to non-use and non-disclosure do not provide opportunities for abuse or inadequate protection.

As a general rule, if you are providing any sensitive information to the other party, you should require the other party to sign a reasonably restrictive NDA *before* exchanging any information. In addition to other concerns regarding protecting business plans and other intellectual property, important state and federal legal protections for trade secrets are lost unless reasonable measures are taken to ensure their confidentiality, including through the consistent use of NDAs.

NDA Hazards

Enforcing NDA obligations requires costly litigation and there is no guarantee you will ever even know about any abuse of your confidential information before it is too late to prevent harm. Consequently, *resist the temptation to over-share confidential information even when an NDA has been signed.*

Additionally, more challenging questions can arise when you are negotiating with a third party that might be a direct or indirect competitor. A designer or manufacturer that works with your direct competitors is one example of an indirect competitor.

In such cases, consider the possibility that an NDA might be wrongfully or unreasonably asserted later to stop you from pursuing a pre-existing plan or to challenge you for an alleged unpermitted disclosure.

As an example, say your company is planning to design and offer a new product and, by coincidence, you meet with a design firm or manufacturer in your industry that might be able to help. You meet, see some designs, but decide not to work with them. If you signed an NDA, when you subsequently launch your own product, that firm might incorrectly assert that you violated the NDA by using confidential information they shared with you.

This risk is tricky and probably warrants consultation with counsel. Strategies for mitigating the risk include (i) refusing to sign the NDA due to the possibility that both parties may be working on potentially competing products or services, or (ii) more commonly, stating explicitly in the NDA that neither party will be precluded from the future development of any products or services currently in design or development, whether or not it learns about similar plans from the other party.

Get Technical Documents and Specifications Early

If negotiations are likely to lead to a deal, start the agreement drafting and review process as soon as reasonably practical. A timely and disciplined approach to deal documentation gets the fullest possible range of issues and information on the table before time is wasted on a potentially bad deal or unsuitable partner. Negotiations that drag out with little urgency around a written agreement can lead to the untimely discovery of deal-stopping issues once agreement drafts finally circulate.

This means pushing for the creation of any technical exhibits, schedules, specifications, or similar documents necessary to document a deal, but only if it also makes sense to do so from the perspective of protecting confidential information, as discussed above.

Chapter Four

DRAFTING

This chapter considers some high level best practices for contract drafting. The next chapter, *Common Contract Terms*, focuses more on the substantive provisions commonly found in commercial agreements.

Clarity

If an overarching theme has been detected yet, hopefully it is that contracts should clarify the rights and obligations of both parties, not confuse them. In cleaning up any agreement, always assume that others will eventually have to read it for any number of reasons:

- Comply with performance or payment obligations.
- Prepare amendments and supplements to the agreement.
- Understand the agreement's term and termination provisions.
- Exercise or pursue appropriate breach or default remedies.

Future readers of an agreement will greatly appreciate being able to understand it. Whether reviewing your own work or a document from the other side, follow these rules:

- Fix unclear or confusing language.

- Remove unnecessary, inapplicable provisions.

- Correct internal inconsistencies.

Drafting Red Flags

It is important to not be intimidated when reviewing drafts originated by the other side, even if they bluster that it is their "standard template" and that they usually do not change it.

As a general rule, if you cannot understand a sentence or paragraph after reading it once or twice, flag it. If someone can explain it, require edits consistent with the explanation. If it cannot be explained, strike it.

Another red flag is any document that seems suspiciously longer than similar types of agreements.

In addition to burdening and possibly confusing future readers, unnecessarily long documents can increase the likelihood of internal inconsistencies and other errors. While some commercial relationships are unavoidably complex, some contracts are too long simply because of bad drafting. "Over-lawyered" templates drafted to cover multiple types of products or services or multiple irrelevant options are common offenders.

While non-lawyers need to be cautious when editing legal "boilerplate," removing wholly irrelevant terms from a bloated template always makes for a more readable document.

More on these issues in the next chapter, *Common Contract Terms,* but in general it is reasonable to take a run at aggressively carving back overly-expansive, one-sided legalese written purely for the other party's benefit.

Completeness

In addition to being clear and concise, contracts need to be complete. While certainly not standardized across all industries and types of agreements, similar legal elements are found across most types of contracts and most contracts are organized using somewhat similar looking headings and sub-headings, like those on the first page of Chapter Five.

Understanding typical contract structure helps one quickly assess how well a document likely addresses key issues:

- Is it clear what the parties intend to accomplish?

- Are their mutual obligations spelled out sufficiently?

- Does the agreement say what should happen if either party fails to perform?

- How and when can it be terminated?

- What happens when it is terminated?

- Which parts of the agreement survive termination?

- How are intellectual property rights addressed?

- How are disputes resolved?

Disputes and disappointments are less likely with contracts that clearly and completely address these issues. Tight agreements discourage meritless disputes by helping keep everyone more honest. Even if completeness requires accepting provisions that cut both ways, it is generally better to choose the devil you know over the devil you do not.

Sometimes a party to a negotiation will balk at detailing performance obligations, timelines, remedies, termination rights, or other terms discussed in the next chapter, *Common Contract Terms*. This is sometimes a clue that they have orally over-promised. Do not be deterred, insist on clear commitments and remedies.

Technical Details

As discussed in the next chapter, technical details are often best addressed in one or more "schedules" or "exhibits" attached at the end of the document. These schedules and exhibits are often captioned "Specifications," "Technical Specifications," "Schematics," "Deliverables," or "Work Order."

Placing schedules and exhibits at the end of the document enhances readability, but doing so is no excuse for less rigorous analysis and drafting, or for signing an agreement before its schedules and exhibits are complete. In fact, schedules and exhibits are often at the heart of one or both parties' obligations and, as such, critical for ensuring proper performance or resolving disputes over performance.

Persons with "subject matter expertise" should review, understand, and take responsibility for complex or technical exhibits, and confirm that each exhibit stands on its own, such that persons with similar expertise will know exactly what it describes and requires.

Understand the Deal

If your role is limited to drafting or editing a contract versus participating in the business discussions to be covered in the contract, get as much background information as possible. Ask who, what, when, where, why, how, how much and a lot of "what ifs" to establish a foundation for your review. Invite yourself to key meetings and conference calls when possible.

Other helpful questions or requests might include:

- Please explain the importance, cost and logic of the transaction.
- How are the negotiations going?
- Are there possible concerns about the partner or the transaction?
- What alternatives were considered?
- What are the technical or industry-specific considerations?
- What are the anticipated implementation processes?
- What are the most important potential challenges or points of failure?

Active Analysis

Carefully reading and analyzing a contract is challenging and requires energy, focus and discipline. Even bad contracts can read well and seem to make sense, especially if you fail to think hard about what might be missing.

The following are some helpful tips for ensuring active analysis:

- Use any background information you requested to identify unaddressed concerns.
- Use a general contract checklist based on customary contract headings and sub-headings to look for important missing provisions. The first page of Chapter 5 provides the general outlines of such a checklist.
- Be alert for passages that overreach or that provide too much flexibility or ambiguity in favor of the other party.
- Imagine different ways in which the relationship could unfold over time and how those different scenarios could or should be addressed.
- Ask yourself whether and how each sentence is relevant, how each sentence relates to the paragraph, how each paragraph relates to the section, and how the section relates to the overall agreement.

Draft Marking

When asked to "provide comments" to the other side's proposed initial draft of an agreement, insist on an editable electronic copy.

All edits by each side should be "marked," i.e., deletions shown as struck text and additions shown as new text. Do not allow the other party to exchange unmarked re-drafts.

Ideally, each "turn" of an edited document from one party back to the other should just show the latest round of edits that have not been agreed to. Documents that continue to show all edits ever made to a document, referred to as "cumulative marked changes," start to look very cluttered, making it harder to identify the latest and most important changes by the other side. Suggest removing mutually accepted marked changes so you can focus on unresolved issues.

Extensive editing is often required to fix a first draft from another party. Never assume that the person who wrote it knew what they were doing, had time to draft it carefully, or had your interests in mind. Mark it up as necessary, but with precision and economy to avoid confusing or irritating the other side. Be ready to explain and justify your changes.

Nitpicking Beats Subservience

If you are new to contract drafting, you may be accused of nitpicking and you may feel awkward about asking a lot of questions. But silently accepting terms you do not understand carries greater risks. It is better to be guarded and cautious than to assume the other party knows what they doing or that they care about your interests.

Review your proposed changes with others on your team whenever possible before sending them to the other side. You might be talked out of an ill-considered edit or realize you missed something. Discussing mark-ups before sending them also gives everyone on the team an opportunity to learn more about the transaction and the proposed agreement.

Although it is always best to get electronic agreements to edit, sometimes it is hard to get anything but a scan or photocopy, locked PDF document, or online terms and conditions. Extensively hand marking documents can motivate the other party to make electronic versions available.

Initial Draft Issues

In reviewing any third-party's proposed agreement, keep in mind that sloppy drafting and one-sided drafting are both *common*. In somewhat rare instances, documents proposed by third parties are so bad that they are simply not a valid starting point.

Several choices present themselves when faced with such a document. The path of least resistance is often to edit extensively until it resembles something you would sign.

If the proposed agreement is so far off that it seems unrealistic as a starting point, consider telling the other party as much, and politely ask that they work with outside counsel to produce a better document.

Starting from Scratch

Depending on timing and resource constraints, a third alternative, and possibly the most practical approach, is to offer to start from scratch with your own document. The other party may simply lack the business and legal sophistication necessary to do better or to even see the problems. Starting from scratch, although burdensome, may be the best way to protect your own interests.

Handwritten Changes in Final Drafts

Handwritten text inserted into, or deletions of text from, the final copy of any agreement must be initialed in each instance by both parties in a manner that clearly reflects acceptance of the changes *by both parties*. Otherwise, it would be easy for the party who has not initialed a change to argue that it is not part of the agreement.

Chapter Five

COMMON CONTRACT TERMS

Introduction

Although every contract is unique, most are likely to contain similar looking headings and address many similar rights and obligations, depending on the type of agreement, the subject matter, and the industry.

Below are some common heading and sub-heading variations that can be used as a high level "contract checklist" when reviewing another party's proposed agreement or creating your own:

Title/Caption
Opening Paragraph
Recitals
Definitions
The Parties' Obligations/
Services
Fees/Pricing/Fees and
Payments
Acceptance
Intellectual Property
Confidentiality

Term and Termination
Termination for Convenience
Termination for Cause/Breach
Effects of Termination
Remedies for Breach
Representations and
Warranties
Disclaimers of Warranties
Limitations of Liabilities
Indemnification
Insurance

Modification and Waiver
Arbitration/Dispute Resolution
Severability
Assignment
Governing Law and Venue
Force Majeure
Entire Agreement
Legal Fees/Legal Expenses
Notices
Survival
Authority/Counterparts

Facts and Circumstances

The objective in this chapter is to highlight common contract provisions and some of the key issues to consider when reviewing or negotiating them.

This discussion is not exhaustive. Every industry and contract-type has its own unique issues that the reader can best learn about by studying similar agreements and consulting with counsel.

Further, the sample contract language chosen throughout this chapter should not be considered optimized for all purposes, nor should it be considered or relied upon as legal advice. In fact, the sample language shown is often more basic and even-handed than language one might expect to see from sophisticated parties with superior negotiating leverage.

Each example is followed by questions and comments intended to highlight key considerations and, in some cases, language variations suggesting how these considerations might be addressed.

As always, each provision of every contract must be drafted and analyzed based on the circumstances. Typical clauses from one agreement to the next can look deceptively similar. Avoid being lulled into complacency when reviewing blocks of familiar looking text. As was highlighted in Chapter Two under *Rules of Contract Interpretation,* important differences can be subtle. A single word like "not" or "except" can reverse the meaning of an entire clause.

Headings and Sections

Not every contract has to include all of the headings shown above or the content associated with them, as discussed below. Sometimes, for example, multiple items are lumped into a single section near the end of an agreement captioned "General" or "Miscellaneous."

Other times, contracts are intentionally silent on one or more issues, such as remedies. As will be discussed in this chapter, tactical omission sometimes makes sense if the other party is likely to insist on very unfavorable language if an issue is called to their attention.

Long versus Short Contracts

In general, less significant or less risky contracts can be shorter, less detailed and even less protective. This is something lawyers, themselves, often fail to appreciate.

"Over-lawyering" agreements by trying to make them overly protective for one party often provokes aggressive drafting responses from the other party or from their counsel. "Drafting wars" between attorneys being paid "by the word" can add unnecessary expenses and delays without producing a better deal.

Over-lawyering a deal or document can also lead to deal failure. The author has cut short negotiations several times where it was clear that the other side's lawyer was too focused on obsessive-compulsive drafting and insufficiently focused on getting a deal done.

Do Not Let the Perfect be the Death of the Good

Lawyers and non-lawyers alike need to remember to not let the perfect be the death of the good when it comes to commercial transactions and other types of deals. While drafting compromises can increase business and financial risks that need to be weighed, the inability to efficiently make deals and conduct business, itself, creates very real business and financial risks in the form of lost opportunities. Success in business often requires being nimble and somewhat risk tolerant.

From a seller's perspective, for example, it is worth considering whether a template agreement that is long or one-sided might unduly hinder new business. A simpler template that produces substantially more revenue may work out better in the long run, even if the likelihood and potential severity of disputes is somewhat greater. The author generally favors this approach, in the belief that rapid business growth means greater profitability and financial resources that will more than offset, and even help pay for, most risks that might arise from somewhat even-handed contractual terms.

Consider Skipping this Chapter

This is *by far* the hardest chapter in the book. It dives into the minutia of contract language. Some of the examples used and the suggested language changes may be challenging and even insufferably boring for readers with little or no experience reviewing actual contractual provisions.

Individuals who are already negotiating contracts or who expect to be doing so soon should coffee-up and proceed. Others might consider skipping this chapter or simply giving it a lighter read.

Title/Caption

The first element of most contracts is its title or caption. Some are short, like *"Licensing Agreement"* or *"Joint Marketing Agreement,"* and others provide additional information, like the parties and the effective date - *"Raw Log Supply Agreement between Big Tree Timber and Straight Board Lumber, Dated December 7, 2017."*

For administrative reasons, it is helpful to use titles that accurately describe the type of relationship involved. Consistent use of titles helps keep things organized by making contracts easier to file and retrieve.

Opening Paragraph/Recitals/Background

Just below the title, most contracts contain an introductory paragraph identifying the parties, their respective addresses, entity types, states of incorporation, and sometimes the agreement's "Effective Date."

Here is a typical opening paragraph:

This Purchase and Supply Agreement ("Agreement"), dated January 27, 2017 (the "Effective Date"), is made between Washington Driftwood Art, Inc. ("Driftwood Art"), incorporated in the state of Washington, and headquartered at 805 State Route 109, Moclips, WA, 98562, and Googly Eyes, Inc. ("Googly Eyes"), incorporated in the state of New Jersey, and headquartered at 101 Industrial Way, Benson, New Jersey, 87625.

Stating an agreement's effective date in the opening paragraph seems more logical and convenient than burying it in the body of the agreement under "Term" or "Definitions," as some drafters prefer.

Recitals or "Whereas" Clauses

Although contracts often omit the caption "Recitals," many still include one or more paragraphs near the beginning that start with the word "Whereas." Recitals or whereas clauses often serve to briefly describe each party's business and the parties' objectives or intentions for entering into the business relationship.

WHEREAS, BuyFromMe.com ("BuyFromMe") operates and maintains a web site, located at www.buyfromme.com (the "BuyFromMe Website"), through which it offers online retail marketing and sales fulfillment of consumer products;

WHEREAS, Magic Hairbrush Co. ("Magic Hairbrush") is a manufacturer of popular, sparkly hairbrushes that wishes to establish a means of online distribution in the United States; and

WHEREAS the Parties wish to advertise and sell Magic Hairbrush Co.'s line of sparkly hairbrushes to customers who visit the BuyFromMe Website;

NOW, THEREFORE, in consideration of the promises and mutual agreements contained herein, and for other good and valuable consideration, the receipt and sufficiency of which is hereby acknowledged, the parties agree as follows: ...

Well-drafted recitals clauses enable any reader of a contract to quickly understand who and what is involved and what the parties intend to do.

Although recitals should not be overly detailed, in more complex or novel agreements it is smart to draft them with an eye toward providing a court, arbitrator, or other third party insights into the parties' intentions and expectations in case issues of misrepresentation, interpretation, or ambiguity arise. As emphasized in Chapter One, *Contract Law*, much of the law of contracts has evolved to guide courts in determining the "intent of the parties" when disputes arise.

Definitions

In many contracts, important words, persons and concepts are "defined" as they are first introduced. Software license agreements, technology services agreements, manufacturing agreements, and other agreements covering sophisticated subject matter commonly include a separate *Definitions* section, where certain terms are defined in one place, in alphabetical order, like the following:

> *Defined Terms. As used herein, the following terms have the following meanings:*
>
> *(a) "Affiliate," whether capitalized or not, means, with respect to a specified person, any person which directly or indirectly controls, is controlled by, or is under common control with the specified person as of the date of this Agreement, for as long as such relationship remains in effect.*
>
> *(b) "BuyFromMe Marks" means trademarks, service marks, and any other such marks developed by BuyFromMe, including "BuyFromMe," "BuyFromMe Now," and "BuyFromMeALot," as well as any links or icons used to direct users from the Magic Hairbrush Website to the BuyFromMe Website.*
>
> *(c) "Confidential Information" means all business information disclosed by one party to the other in connection with this Agreement unless it is or later becomes publicly available through no fault of the other party or it was or later is rightfully developed or obtained by the other party from independent sources free from any duty of confidentiality. Without limiting the generality of the foregoing, Confidential Information shall include Customer Information, and the details of Customer's computer operations, and shall also include Provider's Proprietary Items. Confidential Information shall include the terms of this Agreement, but not*

the fact that this Agreement has been signed, the identity of the parties hereto, or the identity of the products licensed under a Product Schedule. (d) "Copy," whether capitalized or not, means any paper, disk, tape, film, memory device, or other material or object on or in which any words, object code, source code or other symbols are written, recorded or encoded....

This approach to defining key terms works well unless drafters get carried away and define too many terms. The presence of a *Definitions* section sometimes tempts drafters into intellectual hand-holding beyond what is necessary or helpful. If used, a *Definitions* section should make an agreement easier to understand and navigate, not more difficult.

Obligations of the Parties/Services

The critical connection between a clear "obligations" section and robust "remedies" is sometimes hard to appreciate until problems arise. An agreement can include very reassuring remedies for breach, including refunds, setoffs or payment deferrals and rights of termination, but even the most favorable looking remedies can be rendered practically meaningless in the absence of clear performance requirements.

The parties' obligations to each other can appear under a variety of captions like those above and be presented in various ways, although the range of logical choices will sometimes be dictated by common industry practices.

One straight forward approach is to include a caption called "The Parties' Obligations" and sub-captions like "Party A's Obligations" and "Party B's Obligations," followed in each case by text which spells out that party's obligations or directs the reader to where to find them.

Under this approach, for example, Party A's obligations might be to "Pay the Fees described in Schedule A to this Agreement," while Party B's obligations might be to "Perform the Services described in Schedule B, captioned Marketing, Website Hosting and Order Fulfillment Services."

The following is an example of a short "obligations" section:

The Parties' Obligations.

Best Marketing Concepts, Inc. ("BMC"), by its acceptance of this Agreement, agrees to furnish to Subscriber the BMC services described in Schedule A herein (the "Services").

Subscriber agrees to take and to pay for the Services as described in Schedule A, subject to the terms and conditions set forth in this Agreement.

Schedule A in this example assumes a high level of importance. It must be every bit as clear and comprehensive as if the discussion occurred in the main body of the agreement. When the specifics of performance are less complex, it may be best to include them in the body of the agreement, as in this example:

The Parties' Obligations.

ACME Fulfillment will package and ship goods ordered through TechGizmo's online store. To ensure timely and accurate order fulfillment, the parties each agree to perform their respective duties as follows:

TechGizmo's Obligations:

(i) *TechGizmo will ensure that ACME's central warehouse is stocked with sufficient quantities of all goods sold in the online store. TechGizmo bears full responsibility for any order processing delays caused by product shortages. TechGizmo will provide an electronic file to ACME each day by 9:00 p.m. East Coast Time containing the following:*

    a. *complete and accurate name and address of each customer who made purchases;*
    b. *as to each customer, the items purchased, including product code and number of items;*
    c. *each customer's method of shipping selection; and*
    d. *any other special instructions provided by customers.*

ACME Fulfillment's Obligations:

(i) *ACME will receive and process the above described daily file from TechGizmo and ship the products ordered by individual customers to the address provided no later than the next business day, according to the shipping method selected by the customer.*
(ii) *ACME will ensure that all products shipped are packed in a manner reasonably designed to minimize damage in transit; such packaging methods shall be consistent with industry best practices.*
(iii) *ACME will handle all customer inquiries consistent with the Customer Service Standards attached hereto as Exhibit A.*
(iv) *ACME will handle product returns as described in Exhibit B, Product Return Policies and Procedures.*

ACME will take commercially reasonable steps to protect TechGizmo's inventory under its control from all risks of loss or damage and shall carry insurance as described herein under "Insurance." Notwithstanding the foregoing, provided ACME has discharged its duties hereunder with reasonable care, all risk of loss to TechGizmo's inventory shall at all times remain with TechGizmo.

Are the performance obligations of the parties described in sufficient detail here? Answering this question requires thinking through what each party will have to do on a day-to-day basis to make the relationship work. Given the difficulty of anticipating every possible issue, parties to a contract should be alert during the early stages of implementation for additional items to be agreed upon through written amendments or addendums. This is discussed further in Chapter 6, *Implementation* and in Chapter 7, *Amendments and Addendums.*

Anticipate Performance Concerns

However organized, the parties' obligations to each other should be clear, accurate and comprehensive. As already noted, it is easier to make another party perform as you expect if those expectations are in writing. More importantly, if proper performance Is not defined, weak performance likely will not constitute a breach of the agreement, making remedies such as offsets, price reductions, or even termination unavailable. Few things in business are more frustrating than failing to anticipate performance concerns that seem obvious in hindsight.

Careful drafting of the parties' obligations usually requires asking oneself and one's colleagues thoughtful questions about areas of potential disagreement, confusion, mutual mistake, performance shortcomings, and other such concerns that might arise in a new business relationship:

- What is it we are assuming or taking for granted that might be viewed differently by the other party?

- What exactly are we paying for?

- And by omission or explicit exclusion, what should we not expect?

- When must the work or other performance be completed?

- What does completion look like?

- What are the specifications against which successful performance will be measured?

- Where specialized skills are involved, is it important that specific, named personnel perform or supervise the work, or otherwise remain involved and available?

- Are we making assumptions or anticipating conditions, the non-occurrence of which will justify the other party's non-performance, partial performance, or delayed performance?

- Are "change orders" or other performance modifications possible or anticipated? How will they be priced? How will they be prioritized by the performing party?

- Are support services provided? If so, how are they priced and what are the service level standards?

When another party objects to detailing their obligations and when negotiating tensions start to arise around those issues, non-lawyers are sometimes tempted to back down and agree to "high level" performance descriptions. Capitulation to poorly detailed performance obligations usually also involves falling for the other party's oral assurances that the details will be amicably worked out by the parties as they go.

It is perilous to believe that critical performance details will be successfully worked out once the ink is dry. When technical specifications or design elements truly do need to be worked out collaboratively, the best approach is to describe that specification development process in the agreement, bind the parties to a completion timeline, agree that the resulting performance details will become an enforceable addendum to the agreement, and provide for a right of termination in case the parties are unable to timely agree on performance details.

Although there is no perfect substitute for experience, one way to learn techniques for describing performance obligations is to analyze a number of contracts in the same industry.

Technical Specifications

Whenever performance will be highly technical in nature and likely spelled out in an exhibit captioned "Technical Specifications" or something similar, always ensure that those specifications are reviewed and approved by technically competent persons.

If you hire a third party to create a technical "work product" or "deliverable," and the third party builds it according to defective specifications, under contract law, you have nobody but yourself to blame when the work product or deliverable does not work or when it causes harm to others. The manufacturer or other third party has no obligation to identify and correct defects or omissions in technical specifications.

In one real-world example, a device company paid out $1.4 million in an FTC-ordered recall as a result of needlessly defective technical specifications that caused a product to not perform as advertised.

Service Level Agreements

Performance obligations in technology contracts and in various types of services agreements often also include a separate schedule of commitments under the caption "Service Level Standards" or "Service Level Agreement."

These Service Level Agreements, or "SLAs" for short, often include metrics for specific aspects of performance, timelines for responding to "service level failures," and monetary and/or termination penalties for service level failures.

SLAs often cover things like how quickly customer service phones will be answered, the percentage of time that web-based platforms will be available and glitch-free, and the speed with which product returns will be processed for dissatisfied online purchasers.

Consider whether any part of another party's performance can be quantified and how corrective action and fee credits or offsets might be triggered by various types and degrees of performance failures. Consider what penalties will be necessary either to inspire appropriate performance or to compensate for performance failures.

Rights of termination can be triggered based upon a certain number of SLA failures, total "system downtime" within a particular time frame, or some other calculation relevant to a party's potential performance shortcomings.

In the example above involving ACME Fulfillment, SLAs might specify that 99% of orders will be shipped by the following business day, that customer returns will be processed within certain timeframes, that customer calls will be answered within a certain number of seconds, and that customer concerns will be satisfactorily resolved within a certain number of hours or days. Fee credits or offsets might then be triggered by specified percentages of late shipments, percentages of calls returned late or answered slowly, or percentages of customer complaints not timely resolved.

Seller Concerns

It is important for a seller or other party with substantial performance obligations to carefully consider whether the occurrence or non-occurrence of certain assumptions or contingencies might cause performance to become more difficult or costly. If costs of raw materials necessary for performance are volatile, for example, a seller should consider providing for price increases that are tied to increases in raw materials costs. Everything is negotiable prior to signing. That is when to think through assumptions and contingencies.

In contracts for construction projects, these are often called "escalation" clauses, and they often provide for increased compensation to contractors when market prices for certain materials such as cement or lumber increase beyond specified levels. Similar provisions should be considered by any seller where market prices for key materials or components could otherwise make an agreement "uneconomic."

Fees/Pricing/Fees and Payments

Payment clauses generally provide for the time and manner of payment, along with interest in the event of late payments. Here is a typical clause:

> *Client agrees to pay all of the Professional Services Fees described in Schedule B to this Agreement. All invoices for fees charged by Company in connection with the Services shall be due and payable within 30 days from receipt. Interest will accrue at a rate of eighteen percent (18%) per annum (or the maximum rate permitted by applicable law, whichever is lower) on all amounts that are overdue and shall be payable by Client to Company upon demand. No payment shall be deemed overdue if received net 30 of the invoice date. Client agrees to pay all fees and costs of collection, including all attorney fees.*

It is easy to focus too much on the legalese of a "payments" or "fees" clause and miss the key issues. When is payment due and for what? In this example, carefully scrutinize Schedule B, which might say something like the following:

Professional Services Fees

> (a)   *Client agrees to pay the hourly rates described below for Services requested by Client:*
>
> *Senior Developers - $200 per hour*
> *Business Analysts - $175 per hour*
> *Junior Developers - $150 per hour*
> *QA and Testing Engineers - $175 per hour*

> (b)   *Client further agrees that work performed outside of Company's Normal Working Hours shall be billed at 1.5x the rates noted above.*

In this example, it might be wise to suggest language in the Fees paragraph requiring all invoices to detail the work performed by each type of worker. It might also make sense to cap the total amount billed in a given month absent written permission to exceed the cap.

Sometimes payments are required in advance of performance, sometimes after performance, and sometimes along the way as milestones are met. Buyers should generally try to avoid or limit advance payments. If the other party's performance falls short of expectations it is always easier to force corrections or fee reductions before

een made. Another concern worth noting is the fact that prepaid
not recoverable if the other party declares bankruptcy.

hand, the performing party may have legitimate reasons for
partial payment up front, particularly if expensive materials must be
ght, new employees hired, or other lucrative work foregone.

In such cases, the buyer should carefully negotiate milestone payments – i.e.,
an upfront payment to cover materials, progress payments upon the completion
of measureable or otherwise quantifiable milestones, and a final payment upon
completion and "acceptance," a concept discussed below.

The buyer should also insist on clauses suspending payment obligations in the
event of the other party's non-performance. This will be discussed again in Chapter
Five under both *Remedies* and *Force Majeure.*

Acceptance

The term "*Acceptance*" does not appear in every agreement, but when it does, it
can fall under its own heading or under a sub-heading under *Fees and Payments,
Performance,* or a similar heading.

Acceptance refers to a contractually negotiated process in which a party has
the right and obligation to inspect or test whatever the other party has built, designed
or otherwise created, generally before making a specified payment.

If the work product is rejected, specific shortcomings must be identified and the
other party is usually allowed a stated number of days to conform the work product
to the contract specifications.

Acceptance provisions are common in custom software development contracts,
custom manufacturing agreements, industrial design agreements, and other
agreements calling for complex, technically challenging, or creative performance.

Here is an example of what an *Acceptance* clause might look like in a product
design and development agreement:

Buyer's Acceptance:

(a) *By the thirtieth business day from the Effective Date hereof, Company
will deliver to Buyer a working prototype of the "Boxing Buddy"
automated sparring partner, consistent with the Specifications
attached as Exhibit C.*

(b) *Buyer shall have ten days from the date of delivery to test and
inspect the prototype and notify Company in writing whether or not
it accepts the prototype.*

(c) *If Buyer accepts the prototype, Company shall immediately begin
production as described under Company's Obligations.*

(d)   If Buyer rejects the prototype, Buyer must explain its objections in writing, specifically noting in reasonable detail all aspects in which the prototype is inconsistent with the Specifications.

(e)   Following receipt of Buyer's rejection of acceptance as described above, Company shall have twenty days to make the noted corrections or modifications and resubmit the prototype for Buyer's acceptance.

(f)   In the event Buyer determines that previously noted deficiencies have not been corrected or that new deficiencies render the prototype non-compliant with the Specifications, Buyer and Company shall follow steps (d) and (e) above a second time.

(g)   If Company is unable to deliver a prototype meeting the Specifications within the second twenty day cure period, Buyer may declare Company in breach of the Agreement and Company shall return all fees paid by buyer within three business days.

In any situation where it will be important to check whether goods or services conform to specifications, consider incorporating an appropriate *Acceptance* clause. As in the example above, also incorporate a clause like (g) to provide a right of termination if the other party produces non-conforming deliverables after a second or third attempt.

Intellectual Property/Proprietary Rights

Discussions of intellectual property rights come in many forms and under various headings, Including *"Proprietary Rights," "Intellectual Property," "Inventions, Copyrights and Patents," "Content and Marks,"* and *"Ownership of Deliverables."*

Intellectual property issues are among the most difficult for non-lawyers to adequately understand and address. Consider seeking competent counsel to help with any agreement involving the creation, modification or transfer of important intellectual property rights. The scope, nature and complexity of the issues and potential problems surrounding intellectual property rights are concepts that exceed the limits of this book. Some of the general concerns, however, include:

- protecting trade secrets and other proprietary information through appropriate confidentiality and ownership clauses;

- ensuring, where appropriate, that you are the sole owner of any intellectual property being created for you as "work for hire" by the other party;

- clarifying who owns and controls intellectual property rights that arise in the course of the relationship;

- ensuring that any licenses to intellectual property contain all of the appropriate terminology to fully and accurately capture the parties' understanding; and

- requiring the other party to sign documents or take other appropriate steps as appropriate to perfect or protect your intellectual property rights arising under the agreement and giving you a "power of attorney" to sign on the other party's behalf in the event of their unavailability or unwillingness to take such steps.

Here is an intellectual property clause defining Party A's very limited rights to use Party B's intellectual property. In this case, Party A might be subscribing to an online data or research facility operated by Party B:

Company A acknowledges that in conjunction with the Service, it will obtain access to Proprietary Items (as defined below). The Proprietary Items are trade secrets and proprietary property of Company B, having great commercial value to Company B. All Proprietary Items provided to Company A under this Agreement are being provided on a strictly confidential and limited use basis. Company A shall not, except as expressly permitted by this Agreement, directly or indirectly, communicate, publish, display, loan, give or otherwise disclose any Proprietary Item to any person or entity, or permit any person or entity to have access to or possession of any Proprietary Item.

Title to all Proprietary Items and all related patent, copyright, trademark, trade secret, intellectual property and other ownership rights shall be and remain exclusively with Company B, even with respect to such items that were created by Company B specifically for or on behalf of Company A. This Agreement is not an agreement of sale, and no title, patent, copyright, trademark, trade secret, intellectual property or other ownership rights to any Proprietary Items are transferred to Company A by virtue of this Agreement.

Company A agrees to use the Service and the Proprietary Items solely for its own internal use or benefit and not to provide or otherwise make available, in any form, any portion of the Service or any data generated by the Service to any person or organization other than Company A.

"Work for Hire" Issues

Copyright principles are a common source of confusion for inexperienced contract drafters. Many persons intuitively assume, for example, that the act of hiring and paying someone to create written or artistic content automatically transfers ownership of the content created to the party paying for it.

Under copyright law, the person who *creates* "original works of authorship," including literary, dramatic, musical, artistic, and certain other intellectual works, is the copyright owner.

The following is an explanation of "work for hire," or more formally, "work made for hire," from a 2012 publication of the United States Copyright Office on the subject, Circular 09:

> *Copyright law protects a work from the time it is created in a fixed form. From the moment it is set in a print or electronic manuscript, a sound recording, a computer software program, or other such concrete medium, the copyright becomes the property of the author who created it. Only the author or those deriving rights from the author can rightfully claim copyright.*

> *There is, however, an exception to this principle: "works made for hire." If a work is made for hire, an employer is considered the author even if an employee actually created the work. The employer can be a firm, an organization, or an individual.*

The phrase "work made for hire" comes from the U.S. Copyright Act of 1976 and it alters the default rule of copyright ownership. Ordinarily, an author automatically owns the copyright to a work upon its creation. But where "work made for hire" provisions are properly used, the person paying for the work, not the creator, is treated as its author.

One of the largest retailers in the world ran afoul of this concept by failing to protect its rights to years of videotaped footage of company meetings and corporate events. A court determined the footage was owned by the individual videographer who shot it and that the retailer was powerless to stop him from selling the footage online.

Very specific language is required to avoid this outcome under copyright law. The following clause demonstrates the typical "belt-and-suspenders" approach, characterizing the work product as "work for hire" and also providing for a transfer of all intellectual property rights in the event that a court or other "finder of fact" disagrees with the "work for hire" characterization:

Pacific Rim Creative acknowledges and agrees that all Content, Marketing Materials, Video Footage and other content and material created hereunder for Rainy City Walking Sticks ("Works") shall constitute "Work for Hire" and Pacific Rim Creative further acknowledges and agrees that the Works and all rights therein, including but not limited to copyrights or patentable inventions, belong solely to Rainy City Walking Sticks. Should the Works or any part thereof not be considered a work made for hire under applicable law for any reason, Pacific Rim Creative hereby sells, assigns, and transfers to Rainy City Walking Sticks and its successors and assigns, all right, title and interest in and to the copyright in the Works, including any registrations and copyright applications relating to the works and in and to all works based upon, derived from, or incorporating the Works throughout the world.

When in doubt about whether the product of another party's efforts for you might be covered by copyright law, err on the safe side and include robust "work made for hire" or "work for hire" language.

Further, be careful to strike any text that conflicts with the "work for hire" language. Some third party templates with "work for hire" provisions also include language suggesting that the intellectual property rights will be transferred to the purchaser upon payment of all fees owed under the agreement. Such provisions inherently contradict the concept of "work for hire" and should be avoided.

Importantly, California law is somewhat unfriendly to the foregoing suggestions. In particular, little known, frequently disregarded, and apparently rarely enforced California code provisions (Labor Code Section 3351.5(c) and Unemployment Insurance Code Sections 686 and 621(d)) provide that, if an independent contractor agreement includes "work for hire" language, that individual is automatically a "statutory employee." Consult with California counsel if this issue might apply under specific facts.

Patent Law Issues

Similar intellectual property rights issues can arise under patent law. A patent for an invention is the grant of a property right to the inventor, issued by the United States Patent and Trademark Office. A patent grants an inventor the right to exclude others from making, using, offering for sale, or selling the invention in the United States or importing the invention into the United States.

Patents fall into two primary categories, utility patents and design patents:

- Utility patents may be granted to anyone who invents or discovers any new and useful process, machine, article of manufacture, or composition of matter, or any new and useful improvement thereof.

- Design patents may be granted to anyone who invents a new, original, and ornamental design for an article of manufacture.

Virtually any business relationship with a consultant, developer, engineer, or other party in a technical, creative or problem solving capacity is capable of producing rights subject to patent protection and, hence, worth addressing with appropriate language. A product company with a strong negotiating position might be able to impose provisions on an engineering or industrial design firm along the following lines:

Ownership of Deliverables. Industrial Solutions, Inc. acknowledges and agrees that all discoveries, inventions, methods, concepts, know-how processes, products and other technical achievements ("Inventions") that are developed, accomplished, conceived, reduced to practice or contemplated by Industrial Solutions, Inc. during the Term of the Agreement and which are in any way related to Industrial Solutions, Inc.'s work with, for, or on behalf of Big Manufacturer shall be Big Manufacturer's inventions, technical achievements, and absolute property and that all rights of any and every kind related thereto, including intellectual property rights, shall belong solely and completely to Big Manufacturer.

Industrial Solutions, Inc. further agrees, upon the Effective Date of the Agreement, to have its employees sign the form of Intellectual Property Agreement attached as Exhibit B hereto, acknowledging Big Manufacturer's ownership of such intellectual property and agreeing to sign any and all documents requested by Big Manufacturer deemed necessary in its judgment to obtain, maintain, assign, transfer, and otherwise protect and perfect such rights.

Industrial Solutions, Inc. further agrees that, in the event that and to the extent that its officers or employees are unwilling to or unable to sign such documentation necessary to obtain, maintain, assign, transfer and otherwise protect and perfect any or all of Big Manufacturer's intellectual property rights hereunder, Big Manufacturer is and shall be deemed to be attorney-in-fact for such persons and is hereby authorized to sign such documentation on behalf of such persons. Similar provisions shall be included in the Intellectual Property Agreement attached as Exhibit B.

Language like that found in the last paragraph above can be critical for obtaining clean patent registrations when the officers or employees of a design or engineering firm or other paid consultant disappears or is later unwilling to sign inventor assignment documents in favor of the rightful owner. Such documents are *always* required from each inventor by the Patent and Trademark Office. The author has signed on behalf of uncooperative or missing inventors on several occasions, filing copies of the contract language along with the executed assignment document, all without any objection from the Patent and Trademark Office.

Creative and technical experts are often quite sophisticated about protecting their own interests and will often propose language to do so. Most commonly, they will argue that they come to the relationship with substantial intellectual property of their own that is likely to find its way into the "deliverables" and that assigning away such rights exceeds the value of the agreement in question. Proposed language to address their concerns might look like the following:

> *Notwithstanding any other provision of this Agreement to the contrary, this Agreement does not obligate Industrial Solutions, Inc. to assign or offer to assign to Big Manufacturer, Inc. any rights in any invention for which no equipment, supplies, facilities or trade secret information of Big Manufacturer, Inc. was used and which was developed entirely by Industrial Solutions, Inc. prior to the Effective Date of the Agreement ("Retained Intellectual Property Rights"), whether or not incorporated into any Inventions. Industrial Solutions, Inc. agrees to let Big Manufacturer, Inc. use any Retained Intellectual Property Rights that are incorporated into any Inventions in Big Manufacturer's business.*

While this language might look acceptable, allowing a third party to embed their own intellectual property into potentially patentable deliverables could create downstream concerns. A right to "use" embedded intellectual property of another is not the same as a right to sell, assign, or commercialize it, creating a potential ownership "cloud" over the intellectual property. In a financing transaction or merger or sale of the company, for example, it may be impossible to represent and warrant in good faith that no other party has an interest in your intellectual property without first obtaining a costly release from that other party.

At a minimum, where issues like these arise, ensure that the other party grants you a global, unlimited, perpetual, non-exclusive, royalty-free, worldwide license to use, practice and transfer any such inventions.

Even with that suggested fix, the license granted would be "non-exclusive," allowing the other party to share the same "retained intellectual property" with others, including your competitors. This may or may not be a problem.

As noted at the outset, intellectual property issues can be some of the most challenging for non-lawyers. If the stakes are high, consider bringing in competent counsel for assistance.

Confidentiality/Confidential Information

Chapter Three, *Negotiation,* addressed the need to protect confidential information from misuse and disclosure. Before providing sensitive information to another party in a negotiation, require the other party to sign a reasonably restrictive NDA.

The same types of restrictions against misuse and improper disclosure need to be included in any commercial agreement.

Here is a robust example of a *Confidential Information* or *Proprietary Information* clause:

Protection of Proprietary Information. Each party acknowledges that in the course of performing its obligations hereunder, it will receive information ("Proprietary Information") which is confidential or proprietary to the other. Each party shall not use or disclose the other party's Proprietary Information except as contemplated herein, and shall not disclose such Proprietary Information to any third party except to employees who participate directly in the performance of the receiving party's obligations hereunder and disclosures to such employees shall be subject to such employees being bound by written obligations of confidentiality and non-use with respect to the other party's Proprietary Information that are at least as restrictive as the provisions of this Article 11. The parties hereto hereby agree that they shall not use or disclose the other party's Proprietary Information in order to develop products or services that directly or indirectly compete with the disclosing party's products or services. Each party shall protect and safeguard the Proprietary Information of the other party using at least the same degree of care such party uses to protect its own confidential information of like importance, which in any event shall be at least industry standard levels of protection as appropriate for the nature of the Proprietary Information.

Proprietary Information Defined. For purposes of this Agreement, Proprietary Information includes any information and data which is, or should be reasonably understood to be, confidential or proprietary to the disclosing party, which may include, without limitation, information relating to proprietary technical, financial, personnel, marketing, pricing, sales, customer lists, and/or commercial information with respect to the products and services of the parties, as well as ideas, concepts, designs, computer programs (including source code, object code and APIs) and inventions and all record bearing media containing or disclosing such Proprietary Information which are disclosed pursuant to this Agreement, provided however, oral disclosures of Proprietary Information shall only be treated as such for purposes of this Agreement if: (i) at the time of the disclosure the information is identified as Proprietary Information; and (ii) the Proprietary Information is reduced to writing and provided to the receiving party within seven (7) business days of initial disclosure, such writing to identify: (x) the nature of the Proprietary Information; (y) the date and time of disclosure; and (z) the parties present at the time of disclosure.

Permitted Disclosure. Nothing in this Agreement shall prohibit the receiving party from disclosing Proprietary Information of the disclosing party if legally required to do so by judicial or governmental order or in a judicial or governmental proceeding ("Required Disclosure"); provided that the receiving party shall: (i) give the disclosing party reasonable notice of such required disclosure prior to disclosure; (ii) cooperate with the disclosing party in the event that it elects to contest such disclosure or seek a protective order with respect thereto; and (iii) in any event only disclose the exact Proprietary Information, or portion thereof, specifically requested by the Required Disclosure.

In addition to other concerns regarding protecting business plans and other intellectual property, important state and federal legal protections for trade secrets are lost unless reasonable measures are taken to ensure their confidentiality, including through the consistent use of NDAs and appropriate confidentiality provisions in any commercial agreements. Similar protections should always be included in a company's *Terms of Use* or *Terms and Conditions*, whether delivered online or otherwise in connection with its products or services.

Term and Termination

Term and Termination provisions determine when a contract starts and when it ends. They also determine, in many cases, *why and how* it ends.

Before signing a contract, you should have a clear understanding of how long each of the parties will be bound. Negotiating advantageous Term and Termination provisions requires asking oneself questions about the future and about how the relationship might play out.

"What If"

Asking the right termination and other remedy-related questions and addressing them in an agreement requires creative thinking, not unlike the "thought experiments" of philosophers and scientists – essentially, lots of "what if" questions.

In theory, each party is interested in locking up the other party on favorable terms for the longest period that suits that party's interest, ideally with flexible, unilateral rights of termination in case the other party underperforms or a better opportunity comes along.

Unless one of the parties is in a dominant negotiating position, the parties' competing interests and pressures to compromise often drive contracts toward fairly generic Term and Termination clauses.

Auto-Renewal

As a starting point, with many types of agreements, one year contract terms are fairly common, as are provisions stating that the agreement will "auto-renew" for additional one year terms unless either party gives notice of its intent to not renew within a prescribed number of days prior to renewal. Auto-renewal provisions are helpful for preventing situations where parties realize their contract has inadvertently been allowed to lapse, which can raise concerning issues about their respective rights and obligations.

Conversely, realizing belatedly that an undesirable contract has auto-renewed can be equally troubling, as was the case recently with the unhappy customer of a commercial uniform company. In this case, the customer realized just a few days too late that their overpriced Uniform Supply Agreement had just auto-renewed for another five years. The uniform company stubbornly refused to let the customer out of the agreement.

Termination for Convenience

As discussed below, mutual rights to terminate at will or "for convenience" after a short "notice" period are common in some types of contracts and less common in others, often depending on the importance of the relationship to one or both parties. Consulting agreements, for example, often have mutual rights of termination for convenience with little or no notice. Commercial uniform supply agreements are apparently much stickier.

Termination for Breach or Insolvency

Rights to terminate for "cause," or "breach," however, are common, as are rights to terminate if the other party enters bankruptcy or ceases to do business. In fact, the word "breach" commonly only appears in clauses describing rights of termination.

Here is a typical Term and Termination clause:

Term and Termination. The initial term of this Agreement shall begin on the Effective Date and end one year thereafter, unless extended prior to termination by mutual written agreement of the parties (the "Term").

In addition to termination rights elsewhere set forth in this Agreement, this Agreement may be terminated as follows:

Either party may terminate this Agreement at any time during the Term upon thirty (30) days' prior written notice to the other party, if such other party breaches any term or condition of this Agreement and fails to cure such breach within the thirty (30) day cure period.

Either party may terminate this Agreement at any time during the Term, immediately upon written notice to the other party, if such other party ceases to conduct business in the normal course (other than through acquisition or merger, if the successor or survivor continues to perform such party's obligations hereunder), makes an assignment for the benefit of creditors, is liquidated or otherwise dissolved, becomes insolvent, or is adjudicated bankrupt.

In the above example, the term is one year, with no right of "termination for convenience." That means that neither party can terminate unilaterally absent a breach by the other party or other specified occurrence such as insolvency.

And note the phrase "breaches any term or condition of this Agreement." This is a potentially low bar for triggering a right of termination in a situation where rights of termination for convenience were apparently considered undesirable by one or both parties. Any misstep by a party that technically violates the agreement and that cannot be cured within 30 days gives the other party the opportunity to terminate, possibly inflicting harm out of proportion to the other party's breach. The more common practice is to insert the word "material" before the phrase "term or condition" so it is clear that the breach needs to be somewhat substantial.

The following are important questions to ask when drafting or reviewing Term and Termination provisions:

- Will it be important for you to know that you will have the other party's services for a certain period of time and at certain pricing?

- Or does skepticism of the other party warrant a shorter term, or perhaps an initial "test" or "pilot" term?

- Should one party be able to terminate more quickly or easily than the other?

- How quickly and easily can you terminate for the other party's breach?

- What if you are not happy with the other party's performance but they are not quite in breach?

- What if the deal does not turn out to be as profitable as you had hoped?

- If a longer relationship is contemplated, should the contract have a fixed termination date one or more years out, or does the need for flexibility warrant a shorter initial fixed term with successive terms of auto-renewal unless a party opts out?

- If "termination for convenience" is not allowed, what acts or omissions constitute grounds for termination and what is the process?

- What payment obligations are there following termination?

- What other rights, liabilities or obligations survive termination?

When and Why Termination for Convenience is Appropriate

Again, the example above contained no right of termination for convenience, as would be provided by the following passage:

Either party hereto may terminate this Agreement for convenience by providing thirty (30) days notice to the other. In the event of termination, Company A shall only be obligated to pay Company B for services actually rendered up to the date of termination.

Such rights are appropriate for a wide range of services and give the buyer maximum flexibility in managing its business. Although sellers may be less interested in agreeing to such clauses, they are perfectly appropriate where one party is buying common or commoditized goods or services from another. Examples of this might include consulting agreements, as noted above, as well as advertising or advertising placement services, any type of professional services billed on an hourly basis, and any supply relationship where the goods in question are readily available elsewhere.

In general, buyers in fairly liquid markets often have the most to gain from termination for convenience clauses. Easy termination rights provide maximum flexibility to respond to market pricing changes or to broader changes impacting a party's business model.

At the other end of the spectrum, sellers expecting to incur significant up-front costs in an agreement will be far more resistant to flexible rights of termination, at least by the other party. Such costs might be in the form of new plant and equipment or staffing necessary to meet contractual commitments. In such cases, the seller might not expect to break-even financially for several years and an early termination clause would be illogical.

Alternative Right of Termination Triggers

In situations where a seller with significant performance obligations resists "termination for convenience," the buyer might consider other options to clarify and enhance its rights of termination beyond a generic "material breach" provision. Rights of termination drawn more narrowly than for simple convenience but that fall short of actual breach might be more easily negotiated, provided they are specific and reasonable, as in the following example.

> *In addition to the other grounds for termination described herein, Company A shall have the right to terminate this Agreement upon thirty (30) days notice to Company B in the event that Company A has generated sales of Company B's products totaling less than $100,000 in each of two successive calendar quarters.*

This example is intended to show that termination for cause can be defined in any manner the parties agree. Buyers should use creativity in negotiating such provisions to prevent themselves from becoming locked into long and unprofitable or otherwise unsuccessful relationships. Sellers negotiating to avoid broad rights of termination for convenience might use similar creativity to move the discussion in their favor.

Cure Provisions

Other potentially important but often overlooked issues lurk in common "cure" provisions like the 30-day example above.

First, each party should consider whether the stated period is acceptable. Depending on the listed factors that constitute breach in an agreement and the nature of the performance in question, is it too long or not long enough? Buyers, for example, have to consider whether or not it is really okay if the seller cannot meet its obligations for an entire month. On the other hand, a party that could be significantly harmed by termination and that might foresee needing more than 30 days to fix a potential problem might push hard for a 45 day cure period.

Secondly, while "cure" clauses always provide a cure timeframe, they rarely limit the number of times a party may breach and cure, breach and cure. Buyers should always consider negotiating a cap on the number of "cure" periods to 2 or 3 instances, after which any additional breach is grounds for immediate termination.

Lastly, consider explicitly carving out some types of potential breaches from any cure period. Reasonable candidates for an immediate right of termination might include data security breaches, breaches of confidentiality, violations of law or regulation, or violation of third party intellectual property rights.

As suggested by the example above, common bases for termination include bankruptcy, insolvency, or change of control. Carefully consider how such provisions might work to your advantage or disadvantage. If your company is in the development stage and might face financial difficulties, you might not want an insolvency or even a bankruptcy termination trigger in an important contract. If that is not possible, negotiate lenient cure provisions or other protections.

On the other hand, protecting yourself in any agreement with a party that could become insolvent before completing its obligations is tricky and probably warrants consulting with a lawyer, especially where substantial up-front payments or similar commitments are involved.

Change of Control Issues

Lastly, if a change of control is potentially in your future, i.e., a sale of your company's assets or capital stock, strike change of control termination triggers whenever possible and make corresponding fixes as necessary to any "anti-assignment" clauses as well. Negotiating away such provisions in important agreements prior to the closing of a change of control transaction can be both distracting and expensive.

On the other hand, if you suspect the other party might be acquired by somebody you do not want to do business with (i.e., a potential competitor), you may want to insist on a change of control termination right.

These change of control issues are discussed in more detail below under *Assignment.*

Effects of Termination

As just discussed, it is important to know when and how a contract can end. It is often equally important to think through and provide for what should happen post-termination. These questions are frequently addressed under the heading *Effects of Termination.*

Here is a typical clause from a joint marketing agreement:

Effects of Termination. In the event that this Agreement expires or is terminated for any reason, each party shall immediately (a) cease using all Proprietary Information of the other party received pursuant to this Agreement; (b) cease using or displaying all Marks of the other party from its computer systems, storage media and other files or media, and, at the other party's option and to the extent commercially reasonable and permitted under applicable record retention requirements, destroy or deliver to such other party or its designee all tangible items bearing any Marks or containing any Proprietary Information of such other party and all other Proprietary Information within such other party's possession or control; and (c) comply with all other applicable provisions of this Agreement.

And here is a clause from a distribution agreement:

Effect of Termination or Expiration. Upon termination or expiration of this Agreement, Reseller shall discontinue all further promotion, marketing and sales of the Product and Services, provided however, upon such termination or expiration the Reseller will be permitted to sell all Product on hand, provided such sales shall all occur within a period of six (6) months following such termination or expiration.

Sometimes the implications of termination are obvious and fairly routine, as in the above examples. In other cases, though, post-termination winding up or unwinding activities could be more substantial. Here are some examples of these concerns:

- In software agreements, the buyer, or licensee, often agrees to remove versions of the seller's software from all of the buyer's systems at termination of the agreement.

- A video production agreement might require the production company to certify in writing that it has turned over all video footage created for the purchaser and to sign intellectual property assignment agreements in favor of the purchaser.

- Termination of an agreement with a call center provider might require the provider to transfer one or more phone numbers to the next provider and to take other steps to migrate customer service data to the new provider and platform. The price for this cooperation is likely to be much lower if negotiated up front.

- Joint marketing agreements often call for a mutually acceptable communication to customers announcing the end of the relationship and describing the effects, if any, on customers.

- A product distribution agreement might require the return of unsold inventory and provide for a refund for that inventory.

In general, the more important, complex or sensitive a commercial relationship is, the more important it is to think through post termination rights and obligations.

- How will deeply integrated services or systems be unwound or migrated?
- How will intellectual property rights be shared, transferred or otherwise protected?
- How will relationships with mutual customers be managed?
- Should fees be waived or refunded or should liquidated damages be provided for in the event of termination for cause?

The last bullet above alludes to the important idea that post termination rights or obligations can and should vary depending on whether the termination is due to the natural lapsing of an agreement or a party's failure to properly perform.

Termination by Itself is a Weak Remedy

Termination for breach often involves hardships for the party exercising the right. As will be discussed in the next section on *Remedies for Breach,* a party forced to cut its losses because of the other party's non-performance will almost certainly look back at the agreement hoping to find some form of damages, fee clawbacks or other make-whole clauses. Often, that search for relief will be disappointing. Many commercial agreements are woefully silent regarding compensation for another party's poor performance.

As a general rule, sellers of goods or services shy away from exposure to liabilities of any kind for poor performance beyond basic simple repair, replacement, refund, or re-do obligations. As discussed next under *Remedies for Breach,* captions by that name or otherwise mentioning "Remedies" or "Damages" are virtually non-existent in commercial agreements. As discussed below under *Limitations of Liabilities,* most agreements in fact specifically disclaim the kinds of financial harms that are most likely to arise due to a party's poor performance – lost profits, missed market opportunities, and wasted resources.

Effects of Termination Clauses

Consequently, *Effects of Termination* is often one of the only places where a true loss mitigation clause might be accepted, especially if it is logically and directly tied to the non-breaching party's efforts to mitigate its damages.

Sample clauses might look like the following two examples:

Notwithstanding any other provision herein to the contrary, in the event Party A terminates this Agreement pursuant to Section 7(c) because of

Party B's failure to timely launch the Website with all of the functionalities described in Exhibit D, Specifications, Party B shall refund the Development Fee to Party A.

In the event of a termination by Online Marketing Company under Section 11(b) for breach by Cheerful Call Center Company of its obligations under Section 3, Cheerful Call Center shall not be entitled to the Early Termination Fee described in Section 11(a) above and shall, at its own cost, work cooperatively with Online Marketing Company to transfer and assign the Customer 800 Numbers as directed by Online Marketing Company and transfer all Customer Information belonging to Online Marketing Company as directed by Online Marketing Company.

Lastly, *Effects of Termination* clauses should be read in conjunction with their cousin clause – *Survival.* As discussed below, *Survival* clauses generally list, by pertinent section numbers, the clauses of a contract that "survive" the agreement's termination and remain in force. Examples of such clauses are those requiring each party to protect confidential information belonging to the other, provisions dictating the applicable state law and jurisdiction for resolving disputes, and restrictions on the use of each other's intellectual property. It is worth comparing an agreement's *Effects of Termination* clause against its *Survival* clause to ensure they are consistent with each other.

The nature of the relationship, the respective interests of the parties, and their relative negotiating strengths will generally determine what is covered by an *Effects of Termination* clause. The important thing is to go through the exercise of envisioning what a smooth termination would look like and to negotiate clear language consistent with that vision. And where possible, negotiate appropriate language to reduce the impacts of potential default by the other party – the subject of the next section, *Remedies for Breach*.

Remedies for Breach

As noted in the previous section, commercial agreements rarely include captions that include the word "Remedies." This seems largely due to the fact that remedies are often an unpopular subject for at least one of the parties. And although the word "remedies" is found in almost every commercial agreement, it often appears only in very general language limiting or preserving remedies in some way, such as in the following three examples that all preserve the right to "cumulative" remedies:

Except as expressly provided in this Vendor Agreement, any right or remedy hereunder or under applicable law is not exclusive and shall not preclude such party from exercising any other right or remedy that may be available to it.

Any and all rights and remedies of Manufacturing Company upon Your breach or other default under this Agreement will be deemed cumulative and not exclusive of any other right or remedy conferred by this Agreement or by law or equity on Manufacturing Company, and the exercise of any one remedy will not preclude the exercise of any other.

Nonexclusive Remedy. Except as expressly set forth in this Agreement, the exercise by either Party of any of its remedies under this Agreement will be without prejudice to its other remedies under this Agreement or otherwise.

In fact, the only types of agreements that regularly include clauses captioned *Remedies* or *Remedies for Breach* are traditionally one-sided types of agreements such as banking agreements, loan agreements, leases, and security agreements.

Instead, consequences for breach are often addressed directly or indirectly across a number of interrelated sections of an agreement, including *Obligations, Fees, Term and Termination, Consequences of Termination,* and sometimes under *Limitations* clauses.

Across these sections in an agreement, it might be clear when a party can terminate and on what terms, and it might be clear when a buyer is entitled to a fee reduction or credit, but the issue of *paying* damages for poor performance is rarely directly addressed.

Tailored Remedies

Remedies is simply a difficult topic. Rather than have no agreement at all, negotiating parties often seem willing to simply leave a certain amount of risk allocation unaddressed.

A wise contract negotiator, though, should always try to find a way to weave in language that provides not just reasonable rights of termination and rights to fee reductions, credits, or refunds for poor performance, but also, where appropriate, rights to other forms of compensation directly related to the potential harms that would flow from the other party's breach.

The following example provides for substantial compensation rights without using the terms "breach," "remedies," or "damages."

"In the event that Tax Forms, Inc. fails to deliver the Tax Documentation to Financial Institution's customers by the Due Date, Financial Institution shall be free to incur all costs as it deems necessary, both internally and externally, to ensure the delivery of all required tax documentation to its customers and Tax Forms, Inc. hereby agrees to reimburse Financial Institution for all such expenses.

In such case, Financial Institution shall provide monthly reports providing reasonable support for all such reimbursable costs and expenses, including receipts and invoices for the procurement of any third party services and reasonable detail regarding the allocation of internal staff and the full costs associated with such staff. Tax Forms, Inc. shall pay all such amounts within twenty days of the receipt of such support documentation from Financial Institution."

In this case, if the contract also included language elsewhere stating that remedies were cumulative and not exclusive, Financial Institution could be entitled to a refund of any fees paid, recovery of the above described costs and expenses, the right to terminate for breach, and possibly also rights to indemnification from Tax Forms, Inc. in the event of any action by the Internal Revenue Service or harmed customers, all of which would seem perfectly reasonable under the circumstances.

Remedies like those in the above example are extremely difficult to negotiate. Discussions almost invariably become intertwined with counter-proposals for liability caps or other types of restrictions. In this case, the service in question is a good candidate for professional liability insurance or errors and omissions insurance. The *Insurance* discussion below will touch on how proposing insurance provisions in a commercial agreement can help move remedies and indemnification discussions forward.

Liquidated Damages

In any situation where a buyer is contracting for critical products or services and the timely delivery of those products or services per the agreed specifications is imperative, and where the buyer has substantial leverage, it should consider imposing additional remedies in the form of *Liquidated Damages* - a predetermined sum of money that must be paid as damages for failure to perform as required under an agreement. Once liquidated damages are included in a contract, though, the non-breaching party will likely be unable to recover actual damages in excess of the specified amount.

As noted below under *Limitations of Liability,* "punitive damages" are not allowed in contracts and they are not awarded in contract litigation. But "*Liquidated*

Damages" provisions specifying a dollar amount for damages for untimely or inadequate performance are permitted if carefully drafted to avoid characterization as penalties or punitive damages.

In order to not be re-characterized by the other party as a prohibited punitive damages clause in litigation, a *Liquidated Damages* clause must be drafted with careful reference to (i) the facts and circumstances surrounding an agreement, (ii) the harms that would likely flow from a party's non-performance, and (iii) how the specific damages amount or formula relates to those harms. It is also often necessary to correctly recite that estimating "actual" damages at the time of the contract was inherently difficult and that the liquidated damages represent the parties' best efforts at such an estimate.

A court can invalidate a *Liquidated Damages* clause if it finds it was not a reasonable attempt to estimate the potential losses. To best inoculate a clause from challenge, it is important to use clear language and to avoid jargon and boiler plate.

Liquidated Damages clauses are most common in the construction industry, where it is particularly true that "time is money." Property owners and developers can incur additional financing costs and penalties and lose substantial profits when projects are late, not to mention incurring other costs such as keeping engineers, project managers, other contractors, and other field or office personnel on site beyond budgeted completion dates.

Here is a very basic example of a *Liquidated Damages* clause in a construction agreement.

> *"If Contractor fails to complete the work within the contract time or fails to achieve any of the contract milestones, the contractor agrees to pay the owner $1,000 per day as liquidated damages to cover losses, expenses and damages of the owner for each and every day which the contractor fails to achieve completion of the milestone work or the entire project."*

This simple language might be sufficient in the construction industry where *Liquidated Damages* clauses are more common, but in other contexts it would be prudent to include some explanation of why the parties believe the liquidated damages represent reasonable and appropriate compensation to the non-breaching party.

Here is what a liquidated damages clause might look like in the Tax Forms, Inc. example above:

> *"Liquidated Damages. The parties hereby agree that the timely performance by Tax Forms, Inc. of its obligations hereunder is of critical importance to Financial Institution and to its customers, as Financial Institution has strict legal obligations to timely provide the Tax Documentation by the Due Date*

to its millions of customers, who in turn have strict legal obligations to use the Tax Documentation to timely file accurate tax returns with the Internal Revenue Service.

In the event Tax Forms, Inc. fails to timely process and deliver the Tax Documentation, Financial Institution will be required to redirect a large number of its employees to ensure the timely delivery of necessary tax documentation to its customers and to incur substantial costs to identify and retain other third party service providers to assist it in doing so. The parties hereby agree that the exact costs of Financial Institution's efforts to remedy the effects of any such breach by Tax Forms, Inc. are inherently difficult to estimate in advance. In the event, therefore, that Tax Forms, Inc. does not deliver the Tax Documentation to Financial Institution's customers by the Due Date, Tax Forms, Inc. hereby agrees to pay to Financial Institution the amount of $50,000 as Liquidated Damages, which amount both parties agree represents a reasonable estimate of the costs and expenses Financial Institution would need to incur in the event of any such breach by Tax Forms, Inc. Both parties also agree and understand that no part of such amount represents a penalty against Tax Forms, Inc.

A per-day liquidated damages amount might be a more acceptable approach for the other party. In the above example, the $50,000 figure might be replaced with language along the lines of *"$1,000 per day as Liquidated Damages...."*

In essence, a *Liquidated Damages* clause can provide for the same types of damages an injured party to a commercial agreement would argue for in litigation, but without the expenses and delays associated with litigation. Such clauses are rare and difficult to obtain, but worth pursuing in contracts involving substantial fees for complex and time-sensitive performance obligations, particularly where multiple parties are bidding to obtain the work.

Representations and Warranties

Contract drafters should view *Representations and Warranties* clauses as important places to clarify expectations and establish standards that can either expand or restrict performance requirements and hence also expand or restrict potential remedies for performance shortcomings.

Representations can be thought of as assurances of specific facts as of the time of an agreement's signing. Warranties are essentially promises regarding the present and the future, possibly covering a stated period of time.

By way of example, an agreement may require a party to "represent" that they are legally permitted and authorized to enter into the agreement. That same party may also "warrant" that they will perform their duties under the agreement in a manner consistent with the highest standards of the industry.

That said, a party to an agreement could also "warrant" that they are authorized to enter into an agreement and "represent" that the goods delivered thereunder will conform to stated specifications. Representations and warranties are both essentially promises between the parties. No matter what language is used, if the intent is clear, one should expect a court to enforce them in a dispute.

As with consumer product warranties, commercial agreements generally contain specific written or "express" or "limited" warranties that are then whittled back in a later section through legalistic "disclaimers."

And while state and federal laws play a large role in shaping consumer product warranties, in many cases imposing unstated warranties and in other cases invalidating warranty disclaimers, businesses are generally free to negotiate warranties, disclaimers and limitations between themselves without much concern that a court will alter or disregard them.

Note this important caveat, though: in contracts for goods, certain "implied" warranties, like a warranty of "fitness for a particular purpose" may be deemed present in an agreement if not specifically disclaimed between the parties. As noted earlier, sellers of goods should have their sales and distribution template agreements reviewed by UCC counsel.

Before getting into some of the technical jargon found in warranty and warranty disclaimer clauses, let's first look at a very basic *Representations and Warranties* clause in a professional services agreement.

Market Research Company represents and warrants to Internet Retail Company that it will perform the Services described in Schedule A of this Agreement in a competent and professional manner and that it will comply with all applicable laws and regulations in the performance of its obligations. Market Research Company further represents and warrants that, in performing its obligations under the Agreement, it will not violate the intellectual property rights of any third party.

This short paragraph touches on several key points in favor of Internet Retail Company: (i) Market Research Company will do a good job, (ii) Market Research Company will not cause any violations of law that could create difficulties for Internet Retail Company, and (iii) Market Research Company will not violate the intellectual property rights of others in ways that could create difficulties for Internet Retail Company.

As another example, a company providing consumer tax reporting services for a financial institution, for example, might be compelled to make the following warranties:

Tax Forms, Inc. represents and warrants to Financial Institution that: (a) the reports and statements generated by it during the Term of the Agreement shall be compliant with all applicable federal and state tax laws and regulations, (b) the Services shall conform in all material respects to the Documentation and to the other requirements of the Agreement, and (c) all work by Tax Forms, Inc. shall be performed in a professional and workmanlike manner.

Warranties are important because, as triggers for breach claims, they tie directly to remedies such as refunds, price offsets or reductions, performance corrections, early termination, and indemnification.

As a general guide, a buyer of almost any products or services should consider insisting on the following fundamental types of representations and warranties:

- Products or deliverables will conform to detailed descriptions or specifications provided elsewhere in the agreement.

- Any work performed will be performed in a "workmanlike manner consistent with the highest standards/best practices of the industry," in a "commercially reasonable manner," "using a commercially reasonable level of skill and care," or according to other appropriate standards.

- The products or services will comply with all applicable laws and regulations.

- The products or services will not infringe upon the intellectual property rights of any third party.

- In the case of software or software-driven products or services, a warranty against viruses, malware, Trojan horses and other similar concerns.

Those are some of the most basic types of warranties that any reasonable party should be willing to accept and any resistance should be considered a red flag.

Disclaimers/Warranty Disclaimer

Even where reasonable warranty language is accepted, most sophisticated negotiators will seek to cap their warranty exposures and other liabilities by disclaiming a number of specific warranties and excluding or limiting other types of damages. First we'll discuss disclaimers.

Here is a typical warranty disclaimer paragraph, presented as usual in all capital lettering in order to be "conspicuous," the standard required for warranty disclaimers under the UCC and certain case law:

> **Warranty Disclaimer** – *EXCEPT FOR THE WARRANTIES SPECIFICALLY PROVIDED HEREIN, EACH PARTY EXPRESSLY DISCLAIMS ALL OTHER WARRANTIES, EXPRESS OR IMPLIED, INCLUDING, BUT NOT LIMITED TO, THE IMPLIED WARRANTIES OF MERCHANTABILITY AND FITNESS FOR A PARTICULAR PURPOSE, AND ANY IMPLIED WARRANTIES ARISING FROM STATUTE, COURSE OF DEALING, COURSE OF PERFORMANCE OR USAGE OF TRADE AS CONTEMPLATED BY THIS AGREEMENT. PARTY A DOES NOT WARRANT THAT THE PROVISION OF SERVICES WILL BE ERROR-FREE.*

Note in this example that the clause "*EXCEPT FOR THE WARRANTIES SPECIFICALLY PROVIDED HEREIN...*" in the first sentence preserved the explicitly stated warranties in the agreement.

This type of prefatory clause is helpful because, where proper express warranties have been provided elsewhere, it renders the rest of the disclaimer legalese largely irrelevant. And that is important, because here is what the specifically disclaimed warranties in the paragraph mean:

- "Merchantability" is a warranty that generally cannot be disclaimed in consumer transactions; it means that the goods or service must reasonably conform to an ordinary buyer's expectations, i.e., they are what they are purported to be.

- "Fitness for a Particular Purpose" is an implied warranty that can arise when a seller knows the purpose the buyer had in mind and the buyer relies on the seller's expertise to sell the correct product.

Therefore, absent the prefatory "except for..." language, the seller could arguably deliver a product or service that would not conform to an ordinary buyer's expectations and that would not fit the purpose the seller knew the buyer had in mind.

Although a court might "read in" such a prefatory clause if it is absent, adding that language where it is missing is an easy fix and is always appropriate where written warranties have in fact been provided elsewhere. Any argument to the contrary would seem disingenuous or simply uninformed.

Another important point about the above *Warranty Disclaimer* example is that the last sentence should be struck, as the disclaimer of "error free" service presumably would conflict with specifically granted warranties that the work will be performed "accurately," "in a professional and workmanlike manner," or "in conformity with the specifications," for example.

Fixing Typical Disclaimers

Here is a more extreme but still fairly common example of a warranty disclaimer paragraph:

> ***Disclaimers.*** *THE COMPANY SERVICES, PROPERTIES AND RESULTS ARE PROVIDED "AS IS" WITHOUT WARRANTY OF ANY KIND. WITHOUT LIMITING THE FOREGOING, COMPANY AND ITS PARENTS, SUBSIDIARIES, AFFILIATES, RELATED COMPANIES, OFFICERS, DIRECTORS, EMPLOYEES, AGENTS, REPRESENTATIVES, PARTNERS AND LICENSORS (COLLECTIVELY, THE "COMPANY ENTITIES") MAKE NO WARRANTY (I) THAT THE SERVICES OR RESULTS WILL MEET YOUR REQUIREMENTS OR BE UNINTERRUPTED, ERROR FREE OR BUGFREE, (II) REGARDING THE RELIABILITY, TIMELINESS, OR PERFORMANCE OF THE SERVICES, OR (III) THAT ANY ERRORS IN THE SERVICES CAN OR WILL BE CORRECTED. THE COMPANY ENTITIES HEREBY DISCLAIM (FOR ITSELF AND ITS SUPPLIERS) ALL WARRANTIES, WHETHER EXPRESS OR IMPLIED, ORAL OR WRITTEN, INCLUDING WITHOUT LIMITATION, ALL IMPLIED WARRANTIES OF NONINFRINGEMENT, MERCHANTABILITY, TITLE OR FITNESS FOR ANY PARTICULAR PURPOSE AND ALL WARRANTIES ARISING FROM ANY COURSE OF DEALING, COURSE OF PERFORMANCE OR USAGE OF TRADE.*

This example is far more concerning and is the type of fairly outrageous passage that can slip by those who do not know what to look for and who have been lulled into complacency by the pervasiveness of disclaimer language in everyday life.

First, the paragraph absolutely needs prefatory language like that highlighted from the first example, i.e., "*EXCEPT FOR THE WARRANTIES SPECIFICALLY PROVIDED HEREIN. . . .*" Again, that fix assumes that basic representations and warranties have been agreed to along the lines of those discussed above under *Representations and Warranties.*

Second, because Company here is specifically disclaiming that the product will even do what it is supposed to do, the above prefatory language should be expanded to say something like "*AND EXCEPT AS TO ALL RIGHTS AND REMEDIES PROVIDED ELSEWHERE HEREIN.*" The buyer also needs to ensure that the agreement specifically provides for refunds, credits, financial offsets, rights of termination, and so forth for any performance issues related to the Company's product or service.

Third, *"AS IS"* should be deleted. "As is" here means Company is selling and buyer is buying Company's "services, properties and results" in whatever condition they presently exist, and that buyer is accepting the item "with all faults," whether or not immediately apparent. Buyers should push back on "as is" language as commercially inappropriate and potentially confusing in any dispute.

Fourth, the term *"NONINFRINGEMENT"* should be deleted because otherwise Company is indirectly claiming a right to sell stolen or otherwise infringing intellectual property.

Fifth, the term *"TITLE"* should be deleted because otherwise Company is again indirectly claiming a right to sell products or services it does not own.

Lastly, if Company in this case were to refuse to include a *Warranties* clause but still insisted on a robust *Disclaimers* clause, it may be necessary to get more creative with a prefatory clause to the disclaimer paragraph along the lines of *"WITHOUT IN ANY WAY LIMITING COMPANY'S PERFORMANCE OBLIGATIONS DESCRIBED IN SECTION 2, CAPTIONED COMPANY'S OBLIGATIONS...."*

This might not be a perfect solution in the event of a dispute, but it is probably sufficient in this case to keep Company from believing it has cleverly disclaimed all obligations to perform in a commercially reasonable manner.

Generally speaking, in a commercial agreement with otherwise strong warranties, a warranty disclaimer clause that preserves the specifically granted warranties and remedies without directly conflicting or contradictory disclaimers generally should not be much cause for concern. But warranty disclaimer language should be read carefully and anything that does not make sense should be struck or fixed with language changes like those suggested above in order to preserve basic rights and remedies.

It is usually the case that a party can be embarrassed or shamed into deleting nonsensical language like the suggested deletions above. Toward that end, the author is not above asking questions like, *"Why would you insist on the right to sell defective, stolen, or infringing goods?"*

In cases where important fixes are rejected, it would be wise to avoid meaningful commitments, particularly in the form of up-front fees or large termination penalties, and to also have back up options in case "as is" turns out to mean what it implies, "defective."

Limitations/Limitation of Liability

A party's failure to honor its commitments under an agreement, including its representations and warranties, can potentially lead to liabilities far beyond the fees to be charged or earned under the agreement. Each party to every agreement, therefore, needs to consider whether and how such other liabilities should be limited by type and amount. Limiting liabilities is a balancing act – limiting them too severely reduces incentives for competent performance and subjects the buyer to potentially unreasonable risks; not permitting reasonable limitations can prevent an otherwise capable provider of products or services from entering into an agreement.

Here is a typical limitation of liability clause:

> **Limitation of Liability.** *EXCEPT IN THE CASE OF GROSS NEGLIGENCE OR WILLFUL MISCONDUCT, IN NO EVENT SHALL EITHER PARTY BE LIABLE TO THE OTHER PARTY OR ANY THIRD PARTY FOR ANY SPECIAL, EXEMPLARY, PUNITIVE, CONSEQUENTIAL, INCIDENTAL OR OTHER INDIRECT DAMAGES, INCLUDING WITHOUT LIMITATION, LOST PROFITS, EVEN IF ADVISED OF THE POSSIBILITY OF SUCH DAMAGES, IN ANY MANNER ARISING OUT OF OR IN CONNECTION WITH THIS AGREEMENT OR THE BREACH OF ANY TERM, COVENANT, REPRESENTATION, WARRANTY OR OBLIGATION CONTAINED HEREIN. EXCEPT IN THE CASE OF GROSS NEGLIGENCE OR WILFUL MISCONDUCT, AND EXCEPT FOR EACH PARTY'S INDEMNITY OBLIGATIONS SET FORTH ELSEWHERE HEREIN, IN NO EVENT SHALL EITHER PARTY'S LIABILITY TO THE OTHER OR ANY THIRD PARTY EXCEED THE FEES PAID BY PARTY A TO PARTY B FOR THE THREE MONTH PERIOD PRECEEDING THE DATE THE CLAIM AROSE.*

Punitive and Exemplary Damages

Let's first discuss some of the legal jargon in this paragraph. As discussed in Chapter One, *Contract Law*, "punitive" damages are not allowed in contracts, so limitations on them are generally acceptable. "Exemplary" damages are essentially the same as punitive damages and generally disallowed, so that term can be disregarded also.

As discussed in Chapter One, *Contract Law*, punitive damages can be allowed in a contract dispute where a court also agrees to consider tort claims under the same facts. Since any tort claims may need to arise *independently of the contract claims,* a *Limitations* clause like the one above might be found to not restrict damages for tort claims.

In the above *Limitation of Liability* example, it probably helps that this *Limitations* clause does not specifically disallow "tort claims" or "claims sounding in tort," language that is sometimes found in *Limitations* clauses and that might be worth a buyer's effort to delete.

Direct Damages versus Indirect or Special Damages

The key distinctions to focus on in this *Limitations* clause and in most others is really between "direct" damages on the one hand and "consequential," "indirect" or "special" damages on the other, the latter three terms being somewhat interchangeable under the case law.

The following excerpt from a 2016 federal court decision helps explain the sometimes fuzzy differences between direct and consequential damages:

"Rather than turning on foreseeability, the difference between direct and consequential damages depends on whether the damages represent (1) a loss in value of the other party's performance, in which case the damages are direct, or (2) collateral losses following the breach, in which case the damages are consequential…. Direct damages refer to those which the party lost from the contract itself—in other words, the benefit of the bargain—while consequential damages refer to economic harm beyond the immediate scope of the contract…."

"Further, direct damages are the costs of a plaintiff getting what the defendant was supposed to give — the costs of replacing the defendant's performance. Other costs that the plaintiff may not have incurred if the defendant had not breached, but that are not part of what the plaintiff was supposed to get from the defendant, are consequential."

In essence, then, the battle lines around *Limitations* clauses are drawn between (i) direct damages on one hand, for not getting the product or service you paid for and possibly having to replace that product or service, and (ii) all types of indirect damages on the other hand. Indirect damages include things like the following:

■ lost sales or cancelled sales,

■ other types of lost profits,

■ missed opportunities in the market or against competitors, and

■ lost enterprise value from any of the above.

It is worth noting that consequential or indirect damages such as lost profits and lost business opportunities are often far greater than direct damages, hence the interest of sellers in excluding or limiting them.

In the above *Limitation of Liability* example, a reasonable first effort from a buyer's perspective might be to whittle back the scope of the *Limitations* clause by deleting the words "special," "consequential," "incidental," and "other indirect damages," and re-working the language so that part of the clause says:

*IN NO EVENT SHALL EITHER PARTY BE LIABLE TO THE OTHER PARTY
OR ANY THIRD PARTY FOR ANY EXEMPLARY OR PUNITIVE DAMAGES OR
LOST PROFITS....*

The notion that special, consequential, incidental and other forms of indirect damages should always be disclaimed and limited is highly prevalent, but that does not mean you might not succeed at striking those limitations once in a while. Whether or not the effort will be fully successful, analyzing and discussing the types of harms likely to flow from breach can sometimes soften up the other party to considering other alternatives.

Deleting "Gross" and "Willful"

Staying with the *Limitation of Liability* example above, as noted, Party A should probably first try to delete the words "special," "consequential," "incidental," and "other indirect damages" from the *Limitations* clause. This is likely to be met with stiff resistance. If that fails, a good fallback strategy is to delete the words "gross" and "willful" in the phrases words "gross negligence" and "willful misconduct." These phrases are virtually always used in connection with the word "except," meaning in this context that they could open the door to "special," "consequential," "incidental," and "other indirect damages."

To clarify, "negligence" is a much lower standard than "gross negligence," and "misconduct" is a much lower standard than "willful misconduct." And while misconduct is an important concept, contractual issues are more likely to involve the critical distinctions between negligence and gross negligence.

Here are excerpted definitions from Black's Law Dictionary:

Negligence: Negligence is the failure to use such care as a reasonably prudent and careful person would use under similar circumstances.

Gross Negligence: The intentional failure to perform a manifest duty in reckless disregard of the consequences as affecting the life or property of another. It is materially more want of care than constitutes simple inadvertence.

Party A should seek to negotiate away the word "gross" in both places where it appears. Basic negligence is a much easier case to make, increasing the strength of potential indirect damages claims under the "except" clause in the event Party B's negligent performance. When "gross" is deleted, it makes no sense to not delete "willful," and not doing so might hand the other side an *"interpretation"* argument in a dispute.

If *both* instances of the word "gross" are deleted, Party A would be entitled to any indirect damages resulting from Party B's negligence and the amount of any recovery also would not be capped at the amount of three months fees.

If the word "gross" remains in the text, for all practical purposes, the only types of claims available to party A would be direct damages capped at the amount of three months' fees and uncapped rights to indemnification, which are discussed below.

Let's apply some of these principles to the Tax Forms, Inc. example from the *Representations and Warranties* discussion above.

If Tax Forms, Inc. *negligently* fails to properly build and test its systems and thereby fails to produce tax forms for Financial Institution's millions of customers, Financial Institution would be harmed in a number of direct and indirect ways:

- Financial Institution's direct losses might include costs paid by it to deliver the tax forms itself or through another vendor and also to hire additional staff to handle communications with confused and irate customers.

- Financial Institution's special, consequential, incidental, and other indirect harms would include the loss of revenues from customers who closed their accounts in response to the problems, lost opportunities caused by the diversion of employees throughout the organization to deal with the tax documentation crisis, lost future business due to any bad press or social media buzz regarding the tax documentation crisis, and the reduction in Financial Institution's enterprise value resulting from these various indirect harms.

In this example, if Financial Institution was unable to delete the word "gross" in the two places it appears in the *Limitation of Liability* clause, Tax Forms, Inc. would only be liable to Financial Institution for its direct losses and only up to the amount of fees paid in the three months preceding the date the claim arose.

This could be a very bad outcome for Financial Institution, as the indirect harms to it may be substantially greater than the direct harms, and the total liability cap of three months fees could make any recovery hardly worth pursuing.

Financial Institution should have pushed hard for deletion of the word gross and, as discussed in the next section, it also should have negotiated a different liability cap based perhaps on a stated dollar amount tied to an amount and type of insurance that Tax Forms, Inc. was required to maintain during the term of the agreement.

Liability Caps

When a buyer has successfully negotiated reasonable terms under *Warranties* and *Disclaimers,* a seller's final sticking points frequently involve *Limitations* issues like those just discussed, and they often include a proposed maximum liability cap on all damages of all kinds.

At that point, a buyer's goal should be to drive the cap to an appropriately high number by clearly articulating to the other party how its possible non-performance could harm the buyer both directly and indirectly, and how the cap logically ties to those harms.

As discussed under *Insurance* below, raising questions around insurance can help move discussions about liability caps forward by easing concerns about how seller liabilities might actually be funded.

Another thought to hold for now, explained more fully in the next section, is the importance of the language from the *Limitation of Liability* example above, "... *AND EXCEPT FOR EACH PARTY'S INDEMNITY OBLIGATIONS SET FORTH ELSEWHERE HEREIN....*" From a buyer's perspective, any cap on damages should be caveated by similar language so that the seller's indemnification obligations are not inadvertently capped. More on this point below under *Indemnification*.

The interplay among performance obligations, representations and warranties, disclaimers, limitations, and indemnification is like a complex game of whack-a-mole – you fix rights and obligations in one part of an agreement, only to have them cut back or clouded in another part of the agreement.

Here is a high level summary of how to methodically play this game as a buyer:

- Ensure that the other party's obligations are clear under *Obligations*.

- Ensure under *Representations and Warranties* that the other party commits to perform its obligations according to an appropriate standard such as "in a commercially reasonable manner consistent with the highest standards in the industry."

- Make sure that the other party does not unreasonably disclaim its performance obligations under *Disclaimers*; do this by using prefatory language or other caveats that prevent otherwise sweeping warranty disclaimers from applying to the other party's core performance warranties.

- Also under *Disclaimers*, delete any disclaimers that are clearly illogical in light of your expectations for the other party's performance. In the example above, the disclaimers of any warranty of "title" or "non-infringement" were singled out as overreaching.

- Negotiate down the threshold protecting the other party from indirect damages in *Limitations* clauses, as would have been accomplished by deleting the words "gross" and "willful" in the example above.

- Once these drafting goals have been achieved, it is usually a matter of simply agreeing upon an appropriate liability cap, if any. Describing to the other party the types of harms their non-performance could cause and how insurance works in such cases can help to get that number higher.

Regarding the last bullet above, if liability cap discussions get sticky, inquire about the types and amounts of insurance coverage the other party carries. If the other party has a $2 million or $5 million "errors and omissions" or "professional liability" policy applicable to their performance, suggest tying the cap to that number, assuming it is a reasonable number based on the potential liability exposures involved. As discussed below, if the other party does not have appropriate insurance, consider imposing specific insurance requirements and tying the liability cap to the amount of the relevant insurance policy.

Indemnification

The word "indemnify" means to compensate for harm or loss. *Indemnification* clauses generally provide financial protection against lawsuits, government actions, and other *third party claims*, although sometimes they also cover "first party" claims between the parties, as discussed below. *Indemnification* clauses differ widely based on the sophistication and negotiating positions of the parties.

Sample Indemnification Clause

Let's first look at a typical, fairly simple *Indemnification* clause:

> **Indemnification.** *Each party shall defend, indemnify and hold harmless the other party and its affiliates, directors, officers and employees from and against any and all suits, actions, penalties, damages, losses, liabilities, costs (including without limitation, reasonable attorneys' fees), and judgments arising as a result of or in connection with any claim relating to the products and services of the indemnifying party or as a result of or in connection with any breach by the indemnifying party of any of its representations and warranties set forth in this Agreement.*

It is common for *Indemnification* clauses to be "light" like this example, leaving one or more key questions unanswered. Sometimes this is because the parties are unsophisticated; sometimes it is because they both want to keep their document simple and not rack up legal bills.

It is probably also fairly common that a buyer presented with a clause like the one above (i) is comfortable with its vague, open-ended language, (ii) believes the ambiguities might be resolved in the buyer's favor, and (iii) possibly also fears that pushing to address some of the issues discussed below could backfire, resulting in more specific and less advantageous language.

There have been many occasions where the author has "left well enough alone" regarding an *Indemnification* clause like the one above, particularly where pushing for more could bring in more lawyers on the other side and suddenly cause problems not only in the *Indemnification* clause but also under *Representations and Warranties*, *Disclaimers of Warranties*, and *Limitations of Liability*. Things rarely improve when more lawyers are involved on the other side of a deal. Successful contract negotiation often comes down to knowing which battles to pick and when.

With all of that in mind, we will consider the pros and cons of the specific provisions in the sample *Indemnification* clause above.

The words *"Each party..."* mean that it is mutual, applying equally to both parties. As a buyer, offering a mutual *Indemnification* clause is almost always a good strategy for drawing less attention to the whole issue. Although a buyer could certainly be hit with indemnification obligations, sellers are generally far more vulnerable to indemnification claims since liabilities usually arise out of products or services provided by sellers.

The list of indemnitees in the above *Indemnification* example is fairly complete, i.e., *"...the other party and its affiliates, directors, officers and employees...."* Sometimes "agents" and "contractors" are also explicitly covered.

The list of covered harms is also fairly complete, i.e., *"from and against any and all suits, actions, penalties, damages, losses, liabilities, costs (including without limitation, reasonable attorneys' fees), and judgments arising as a result of or in connection with any claim relating to the products and services of the indemnifying party or as a result of or in connection with any breach by the indemnifying party of any of its representations and warranties set forth in this Agreement."*

This litany of covered harms is arguably the heart of the clause. Clearly the indemnifying party is required, one way or another, to pay the indemnified party's costs, expenses, losses, damages, and judgments relating to any third party claims caused by, arising out of, or relating to the indemnifying party's products or services or its breach of its representations or warranties. This would include any civil lawsuits, arbitrations, government civil and administrative actions, and other such actions.

The phrase, *"arising as a result of or in connection with any claim relating to the products and services of the indemnifying party,"* is suitably broad, especially in conjunction with the important phrase "... or *as a result of or in connection with any breach by the indemnifying party of any of its representations and warranties set forth in this Agreement."* Another common phrase is *"arising as a result of or in connection with the indemnifying party's performance of its obligations under the Agreement."*

These language subtleties are not tested and interpreted enough in courts to draw definitive conclusions on what is going to work best consistently, but indemnification triggers that relate broadly to the indemnifying party's conduct, obligations, and representations and warranties should generally be sufficient. Once again, if indemnification might be an important issue in a contract, it is probably worth talking with experienced counsel.

Duty to Defend

The word "defend" in the first line of the above *Indemnification* clause is very important. It implies a duty to immediately and actively defend or pay for the defense of any claim from the beginning of the claim or litigation. Thus, the indemnified party can theoretically avoid ever paying any legal fees or other litigation expenses out of pocket.

Absent a duty to defend in an Indemnification clause, an indemnifying party might argue that the indemnified party is only entitled to be indemnified for its costs, expenses, and other losses at the end of a litigation or other resolution of the claims.

The "Merits"

It is also worth noting that, under the above *Indemnification* clause, the indemnifying party clearly has to defend any covered claim, regardless of whether the claims have any merit. That means that even "frivolous" third party claims would be covered.

And even if the word *defend* was not included in the sample language, the indemnifying party would still have to subsequently pay the indemnified party's *costs*, including *reasonable attorney's fees*, regardless of any determination of the "merits" of a claim.

That is how *Indemnification* clauses usually work – they allocate the risk of any claims arising out of a party's performance, products, services, and/or breaches, regardless of the merits of such claims.

More sophisticated parties sometimes try to condition indemnification on the merits. A seller might, for example, try to rewrite the example above by deleting the words "defend," "hold harmless," "suits, actions," and a few other key words, and by adding new text like the underlined text shown in this revised example:

> **Indemnification.** *Each party shall indemnify the other party and its affiliates, directors, officers and employees from and against any and all penalties, damages, losses, liabilities, costs (including without limitation, reasonable attorneys' fees), and judgments arising as a result of or in connection with any* <u>*successfully adjudicated*</u> *claim relating to (i) the products and services of the indemnifying party or (ii) any breach by the indemnifying party of any of its representations and warranties set forth in this Agreement.*

Under this revised example, indemnification obligations would arise only after a trial or other adjudication in which either (i) the indemnifying party's products or services themselves or (ii) the falsity of the indemnifying party's breach of its representations or warranties are proven to have caused harm or some other liability.

Language like this would be highly unusual and should be resisted whenever you are likely to be the indemnified party.

More reasonable demands from a seller might be to insert language precluding indemnification obligations if the claims or liabilities in question were caused by the negligence or misconduct of the indemnified party. This usually involves substantially simpler edits by a seller and is often more acceptable to a buyer.

Here is an example with a reasonable carve-out for an indemnified party's negligence or misconduct:

> **Indemnification.** *Each party shall defend, indemnify and hold harmless the other party and its affiliates, directors, officers and employees from and against any and all suits, actions, penalties, damages, losses, liabilities, costs (including without limitation, reasonable attorneys' fees), and judgments (i) arising as a result of or in connection with any claim relating to the products and services of the indemnifying party, <u>except where caused by an indemnified party's own negligence or misconduct,</u> or (ii) as a result of any breach by the indemnifying party of any of its representations and warranties set forth in this Agreement.*

When representing a seller, the author frequently argues for changes like these to prevent indemnification claims for harms actually caused by the buyer.

First Party Claims

A key ambiguity in the above sample *Indemnification* clause, though, is whether it is intended to cover "first party" claims between the parties, or just third party claims. The language *"… all suits, actions,… damages,… losses,… in connection with any claim…"* is ambiguous on this point.

The question could probably go either way in many jurisdictions, but the better and more likely answer is that the clause only covers third party claims. Courts have held that *Indemnification* clauses are to be "strictly construed" and some courts addressing the issue have said "first party" coverage requires specific language referencing "first party" claims or "claims between the parties," or unique circumstances indicating that, without such coverage, the overall clause would make no sense. The example above meets none of these tests.

To clarify the language regarding first party claims *in the negative,* one would only need to insert the words *"third party"* in front of the word *"claims."* To clarify that the clause applied to first party claims, one could add the words *"first party or third party"* in front of the word *"claims."*

As a negotiating matter, in cases involving sophisticated parties, adding specific language to clearly cover first party claims in an *Indemnification* clause would be a tough sell. The best objections would be that such language is "non-standard," which it is, and that it is also not necessary because a party can always sue the other party for damages in the event of a breach.

On the other hand, the best reason for pushing for first party claims coverage is the fact that the words *"including reasonable attorneys' fees"* are almost always found in *Indemnification* clauses. Under American law, the winner in litigation is rarely entitled to its litigation costs and expenses from the other party, including attorneys' fees, absent clear contractual language providing for them. Sneaking "first party claims" into an *Indemnification* is one of the better ways of making another party pay you for suing them for breach; the other way is a "prevailing party" clause, as discussed below under *Legal Expenses/Legal Fees.*

Notice, Control of Defense and Settlement, Limitations

We will now consider some additional "bells and whistles" that are often found in *Indemnification* clauses. They fall into the following categories, ordered roughly from more common to less common:

- Indemnification Procedures/Notice Provisions
- Obligations to Defend/Merit Issues
- Rights to Control Settlement
- Applicability of Limitations Cap
- Statutes of Limitation
- Sole Remedy

Assume the next paragraph follows the above sample *Indemnification* paragraph:

The party to be indemnified hereunder shall (i) promptly notify the indemnifying party in writing of any indemnifiable claim and give such party the opportunity to defend or negotiate a settlement of the claim at the indemnifying party's expense, and (ii) cooperate fully with the indemnifying party, at the indemnifying party's expense, in defending or settling the claim. Notwithstanding the foregoing sentence, the party being indemnified hereunder may participate, at its own expense, in any proceedings or negotiations related to such defense or settlement with its own counsel, provided that such counsel does not interfere with the defense of any claim.

This short paragraph covers the first three of the bullet points above. The indemnified party must give timely notice and the indemnifying party clearly has the right to control both the defense of any claim and the settlement of any claim. Failure to provide timely notice of a claim under these terms could raise serious questions about whether the indemnifying party is wholly or partly released from its indemnification obligations. This is particularly true if a credible claim can be asserted that lack of timely notice somehow jeopardized or compromised the indemnifying party's ability to resolve the matter more cost effectively. When required, providing timely written notice to an indemnifying party (and any applicable insurer) is critically important.

It is very common for a party with substantial indemnification exposure to insert language giving that party the right to control and manage any litigation relating to an indemnifiable claim, particularly where the claims are likely to be within that party's expertise, such as intellectual property infringement, product liability, or highly specialized regulatory matters regarding its products or services.

Whenever the other party would probably do a better job fighting third party claims, it is common and wise to accept language allowing the indemnifying party to "control the defense." Big companies almost always demand this and it is usually the right choice given their larger legal budgets and stronger subject matter expertise.

Where smaller, less sophisticated companies are demanding to control indemnification defense, greater skepticism is warranted. And certainly, any time there is a risk the other party might conduct a poor defense and then be unable to honor its indemnification obligations, push back against transferring rights to defend.

Hidden Indemnification Caps

It is rare to see a financial cap on indemnification obligations in an *Indemnification* clause itself. A buyer should try to negotiate to remove any such cap or increase it to a dollar amount that is not concerning. A cap of $5 million or $10 million in today's dollars, for example, would be acceptable in many agreements where product liability or intellectual property claims are unlikely.

But caps on indemnification usually lurk much more stealthily in *Limitations* or *Limitation of Liability* clauses. A *Limitation of Liability* clause like the following, for example, could be argued to cap indemnification obligations at a very low level:

EXCEPT IN THE CASE OF GROSS NEGLIGENCE OR WILLFUL MISCONDUCT, IN NO EVENT SHALL EITHER PARTY'S LIABILITY HEREUNDER TO THE OTHER OR ANY THIRD PARTY EXCEED THE FEES PAID BY PARTY A TO PARTY B FOR THE THREE MONTH PERIOD PRECEEDING THE DATE THE CLAIM AROSE.

In this example, the words *"IN NO EVENT"* and *"OR ANY THIRD PARTY"* would seem to encompass indemnification liabilities, whether intentionally or not. Although indemnification obligations could be argued to be purely contractual commitments and not liabilities, they are also arguably a form of liability running from one party to the other. The presence of the phrase "any third party" in the example reinforces the suggestion that the cap is intended to cover indemnification of third party claims, even though the term "indemnification" is not used.

Finding their seller's indemnification obligations capped so low in the event of a claim would likely surprise most buyers. The problem for many contract reviewers is that they do not tie the above type of liability cap to the protections described under *Indemnification.* The two clauses are often separated by pages in agreements and the indemnification language usually reads as a wholly separate matter to both lawyers and non-lawyers alike.

Fortunately there is an easy fix. And it needs to go into almost every commercial agreement. In the above language, simply insert the following phrase before the words *"IN NO EVENT":*

"AND EXCEPT FOR EACH PARTY'S INDEMNITY OBLIGATIONS SET FORTH ELSEWHERE HEREIN,"

This is another handy use of the word *"except"* in commercial agreements, and this fix is often accepted without objection, so do not be reluctant to propose it.

Sometimes a *Limitations of Liability* clause will even include specific language referencing indemnification obligations as being subject to the liability cap. In such cases, a buyer should try to strike the indemnification reference and replace it with the "except" clause above.

This, too, often works. But if it fails, the next line of defense is to negotiate a higher overall cap. If that fails, negotiate a special cap for indemnification that is higher than the general damages cap.

As described in the next section, requiring the seller to maintain appropriate insurance coverages and then tying caps to that coverage often works well.

Exclusive Remedy Language

Lastly, buyers should watch for and try to strike language in *Indemnification* clauses that says anything along the lines of *"and the Indemnified Party hereby agrees that the remedies described herein shall be the sole and exclusive remedies to which such Party shall be entitled under this Agreement."*

As noted earlier, indemnification protections often do not cover "first party" direct or indirect damages, so an exclusivity clause would not make sense where these other types of harms *plus* indemnifiable third party claims might flow from the other party's breaches.

Insurance

Insurance clauses are not found in every agreement. They are most important where a party's performance or non-performance could result in potential damages and indemnification obligations beyond the indemnifying party's ability to pay, particularly in the event of insolvency or bankruptcy.

When insured risk allocation is important, the *Insurance* clause should include several key elements, including:

- appropriate coverage amounts,
- appropriate types of coverage,
- correct "additional insured" language, and
- appropriate notification of cancellation provisions.

Here is a clause imposing identical coverage requirements on both parties to a medical device distribution agreement, followed by commentary:

> *Insurance. Within ten (10) days of execution of the Agreement, and upon request throughout the term of this Agreement, each party will provide the other party with a certificate of insurance evidencing (i) the name of a reputable insurance company; (ii) the policy number; (iii) at least $2,000,000 of general liability and product liability coverage (to be increased to $5,000,000 once Reseller has 10,000 Concurrent Users activated); (iv) that the other party is an additional insured, on a primary basis, for both ongoing operations and completed operations and (v) that Company or Reseller, as the case may be, will receive at least thirty (30) days prior written notice of any modification, cancellation or non-renewal of such coverage, but in no case later than three business days of receipt of notice of cancellation, modification or non-renewal from the insurance company.*

Certificate of Insurance

If insurance is important, requiring a certificate of insurance can help ensure that the requirement is not ignored. Insurance companies regularly produce these, so it is a reasonable request.

Note in this example that the insurance coverage amount was negotiated to increase as the commercial arrangement evolved. The other party to this agreement originally balked at the higher amount but was willing to accept the phased approach, an excellent negotiating tactic for obtaining higher coverage limits.

Additional Insured, Notice, Primary versus Excess

This example also includes a common "additional insured" requirement. An "additional insured" is a person or organization named in another person's or organization's insurance policy as also being covered by the financial protections of the insurance policy.

Here are several key points about the additional insured language shown above:

- First, *absent a contractual requirement* that a party be made an "additional insured," that status might not be honored by the insurance carrier in the event of a claim, even if a certificate of insurance states that the party is an additional ensured. That is because insurance endorsements to underlying policies usually provide additional insured status only when "required by a written contract."

- Second, make sure the additional insured coverage is "primary," otherwise it might be on an "excess basis" only, meaning after payouts by the indemnified party's insurer.

- Third, many potential claims could arrive after an agreement has been terminated; absent language requiring coverage for "completed operations," coverage for such post-termination claims could be denied.

Coverage Types

Lastly, the sample language above specifically requires product liability coverage. Depending on the nature of the commercial relationship, it is important to require the correct coverage types. Here are some of the most common:

- General liability coverage is important if a party's employees or agents will be present and performing services or otherwise performing under the agreement at the other party's facilities or inviting the other party's employees or agents to its own facilities.

- Errors and omissions coverage is important if the other party is performing any kind of professional services, including designing, building, hosting or maintaining products, services or systems, or handling customer transactions.

- Privacy and network and data security coverage is important if the other party will be handling or have access to personal data, or designing, building, hosting or maintaining systems handling personal data.

- Media coverage is important if the other party will be serving in any capacity as a publisher, broadcaster, content creator or manager, or otherwise handling media functions.

- Intellectual property coverage is among the most expensive but would be valuable if the other party's products, services or other performance under an agreement could create substantial risk of third party infringement claims.

Dealing with Objections

When insurance requirements are critical and the other party objects, it is often most helpful to start the discussion by asking why. If the answer is that they do not carry the type of insurance in question, the next step is to ask them to look into the cost and availability of the coverages in question.

A good insurance broker or agent is likely to convince them that the requested coverage would be wise to have in any event, and often the cost of coverage is less than feared. Insurance companies are accustomed to providing "additional insured" status to contract parties and are surprisingly cooperative in doing so in response to contractual requirements.

If the other party is stubborn, one tactic is to explain that "the commercially reasonable practice" is for each party to insure against the risks its performance creates, since the other party is often not in a position to buy that insurance for itself. Whether or not true in the specific case, this has a reasonable ring and often wins the day.

Use Professionals

One of the best tips for getting an insurance clause right is to run it by a professional insurance broker or agent, especially if the issues are complex or the other side is pushing for confusing language. Insurance brokers are very familiar with these issues, they usually give excellent free advice, and the information and guidance they provide can be very useful in moving difficult negotiations forward.

A Poor Substitute for Good Judgment

As important as insurance can be, it is no substitute for good judgment and strong drafting when entering into commercial agreements. "Additional insured" coverage is usually only going to cover third party claims and certain types of direct harms. It provides no coverage for most types of indirect losses a party can suffer under a bad agreement with the wrong person or company.

The "Insurance" Chip

In cases where having an *Insurance* clause is not critical, including one in a first draft can provide a possible bargaining chip for more important concessions. Smaller companies often do not carry comprehensive insurance coverage types or substantial coverage amounts. Sometimes, a potentially burdensome but arguably unnecessary *Insurance* clause can be a good chip to trade for more important terms.

Modification and Waiver

Modification and waiver are two different but somewhat related concepts. As a result, they are often addressed under the same heading. But not always. *Waiver and Modification* clauses are rarely sources of concern.

Here is an example of a reasonably robust *Modification and Waiver* clause:

> *No failure, delay or other course of conduct on the part of either party in exercising any right, power or remedy under this Agreement shall operate as a waiver of such right, power or remedy, nor shall any single or partial exercise of any such right, power or remedy preclude any other right, power or remedy. Unless otherwise specified, any amendment, supplement or modification of or to any provision of this Agreement, any waiver of any provision of this Agreement and any consent to any departure by the parties from the terms of this Agreement, shall be effective only if it is made or given in writing and signed by authorized signatories from both parties.*

Waiver

The first sentence above deals with "waiver," or, more accurately, the disclaiming of "waiver." In this context, waiver means that a party, through its conduct or communications, has forgiven, or "waived," the other party's performance shortcomings.

The above fairly standard language allows each party to exercise its best self-interested judgment in the face of the other party's faltering or failing performance. The injured party does not need to resort to its most strict remedies immediately. Waiver language along these lines is helpful and should always be included in commercial agreements.

Modification

The second sentence in the above example simply clarifies that, once an agreement has been negotiated and signed, any amendment, addendum or other modification should also be negotiated and signed. This language reduces the possibility that less formal written or oral communications between individuals at varying levels of responsibility in the parties' organizations will later be viewed as amendments to the original agreement.

While this language is common and should be included for both parties' protection, it highlights the importance of ensuring that each party's obligations are clearly and comprehensively described, along with all other rights, remedies and obligations discussed above.

Arbitration

Except in industries like construction, where arbitration clauses are the norm, inclusion of an *Arbitration* clause is still a matter of personal preference in many situations, or perhaps more accurately, the preference of any counsel involved in drafting or negotiating the agreement in question.

As with any other contractual provision, parties also have broad latitude in drafting arbitration clauses. Some of the biggest issues are whether an *Arbitration* clause is mandatory or voluntary, appealable or non-appealable, and whether it is applicable to all issues under an agreement or only to certain issues.

Here is a typical *Arbitration* clause:

If any dispute arises concerning the performance, interpretation, or enforcement of this Agreement, the parties hereto agree that such matter shall be determined by arbitration, upon the written request of one party given to the other. Such arbitration shall be conducted in King County, Washington, and shall be in accordance with the American Arbitration Association under its Commercial Arbitration Rules then in effect. Any award under such arbitration, including any award for damages, may be entered in any court having jurisdiction thereof. In the event of any litigation or arbitration under this Agreement, the prevailing party shall be entitled to reasonable attorney's fees and costs in addition to other relief.

In this very typical arbitration clause, arbitration is both mandatory and binding, with no right to appeal.

In theory, arbitration and its cousin mediation are supposed to be faster, less expensive, less formal, and less public means of equitably resolving disputes. While definitely faster and less expensive than full blown litigation, arbitration has evolved into a more formalistic process than originally envisioned, incorporating analogs to expensive and time consuming processes found in civil litigation, but without some of the key benefits of litigation.

In the author's view, the trade-off for potentially greater speed and lower cost often comes with risks of reduced decision-making quality, predictability, and tactical flexibility.

Splitting the Baby

Among other concerns, it is logical to assume that an arbitrator with no expectation of being reviewed by a judge is likely to be less robust in their analysis and application of the law than an experienced judge whose decision would be open to review and reversal by an appellate court. Because arbitrators operate with such freedom, some express a concern that they tend to "split the baby" – i.e., give something to both parties regardless of the actual merits of the case.

Process Details and Exceptions

Arbitration clauses vary greatly in how they are written and what they cover. The following example provides: (i) more detail regarding the arbitration rules and procedures, (ii) an exception for "equitable relief," and (iii) a specific waiver of special or consequential damages.

> *Arbitration. Notwithstanding the foregoing, except with respect to enforcing claims for injunctive or equitable relief, any dispute, claim or controversy arising out of or relating in any way to this Agreement, any other aspect of the relationship hereunder between Manufacturer and Customer or their respective affiliates and subsidiaries, the interpretation, application, enforcement, breach, termination or validity thereof (including, without limitation, any claim of inducement of this Agreement by fraud and a determination of the scope or applicability of this agreement to arbitrate), or its subject matter (collectively, "Disputes") shall be determined by binding arbitration before one arbitrator.*

> *The arbitration shall be administered by JAMS conducted in accordance with the expedited procedures set forth in the JAMS Comprehensive Arbitration Rules and Procedures as those Rules exist on the effective date of this Agreement, including Rules 16.1 and 16.2 of those Rules. Notwithstanding anything to the contrary in this Agreement, the Federal Arbitration Act shall govern the arbitrability of all Disputes. The arbitration shall be held in King County, Washington, and it shall be conducted in the English language. The parties shall maintain the confidential nature of*

the arbitration proceeding and any award, including the hearing, except as may be necessary to prepare for or conduct the arbitration hearing on the merits, or except as may be necessary in connection with a court application for a preliminary remedy, a judicial challenge to an award or its enforcement, or unless otherwise required by law or judicial decision.

The arbitrator shall have authority to award compensatory damages only and shall not award any punitive, special or consequential damages, and the parties waive any right to recover any such damages. Judgment on any award in arbitration may be entered in any court of competent jurisdiction. Notwithstanding the above, each party shall have recourse to any court of competent jurisdiction to enforce claims for injunctive and other equitable relief.

Equitable Relief

Equitable relief means *everything but money damages*. It includes things like forcing a party to: (i) perform its obligations, (ii) return confidential information or (iii) stop doing something. In litigated matters, equitable relief often comes in the form of a *"Permanent Injunction"* or a *"Temporary Injunction."*

In the author's view, buyers should push for an "equitable relief" exclusion like the one in the sample *Arbitration* clause above. These matters seem better suited to civil litigation than arbitration. But reasonable minds certainly differ. Others believe arbitrators are capable of quickly fashioning creative equitable relief. Litigation strategies and other dispute resolution tactics are discussed further in Chapter 8, *Dispute Resolution*.

Tactical Concerns

When arbitration is mandatory, tactical flexibility is lost. Sometimes the potential hammer of litigation is the only tool that will reliably compel a non-performing party to either perform or pay up. When the law and facts are on your side, the threat to litigate can be more intimidating and more effective than a threat to arbitrate or mediate.

Even if an agreement does not contain an *Arbitration* clause, parties in dispute can still agree to either arbitration or mediation. This may be mutually desirable, for example, if both parties wish to keep the existence or nature of the dispute confidential.

Another possibility for closing the gap a bit between arbitration and litigation is negotiating for any arbitration decision to be appealable. In many states, that is likely to require very specific language along the following lines:

The arbitrator(s) must provide to the parties a written award including factual findings and the reasons for their decision. The arbitrators shall not have the power to commit errors of law or legal reasoning. The award is subject to review for legal error, confirmation, correction or vacatur in the state courts of Washington.

Severability

Almost every contract contains a *Severability* clause, also sometimes called a "*Savings Clause.*" These clauses are relatively self-explanatory and are rarely problematic in commercial agreements or disputes. The following are two examples of *Severability* clauses:

Severability. If any provision of these Terms is determined to be illegal or unenforceable, that provision will be limited or eliminated to the minimum extent necessary so that these Terms will otherwise remain in full force and effect and enforceable.

Severability. In the event that any part of this Agreement is found to be unenforceable, the remainder shall continue in effect and such part shall be changed and interpreted so as to best accomplish the objectives of such part to the extent permissible by law and consistent with the intent of the parties as of the Effective Date.

However written, the purpose of a *Severability* clause is to allow a specific illegal or otherwise unenforceable term to be "severed" or somehow modified in the narrowest or least impactful manner possible consistent with the intent of the parties.

Frustration of an Essential Purpose

The primary concern worth pointing out regarding *Severability* clauses is the possibility that a term or provision at the heart of the deal for one or the other party could be deemed or recognized to be invalid but the *Severability* clause continues to impose full performance obligations on the party most harmed by such invalidation. This could happen, for example, if part of a party's performance itself were deemed to violate a regulatory prohibition. Should the contract still continue in effect, even though part of one party's performance is prohibited?

Drafting to account for such unintended consequences, sometimes called "frustration of an essential purpose" of an agreement, is rarely done. The example below does a better job anticipating this concern, but still addresses it indirectly:

Severability. If for any reason any provision of this Agreement shall be determined to be invalid or inoperative, (i) that provision shall be deemed amended to achieve as nearly as possible the same economic effect as the original provision, and (ii) the legality, validity and enforceability of the remaining provisions of this Agreement shall not be affected or impaired thereby.

The language *"that provision shall be deemed amended to achieve as nearly as possible the same economic effect..."* acknowledges that changes to the terms could alter the economics of the deal, one or both parties' "benefit of the bargain," but it does not provide a hard fix, such as a right of termination.

If a contract contains potentially questionable provisions that might come under judicial or regulatory scrutiny or even under a party's internal "reconsideration," creative drafting might be in order. One solution would be to simply add a right of termination to the *Severability* clause along these lines:

Notwithstanding the foregoing, in the event any provision of this Agreement shall be determined to be invalid or inoperative, and any necessary remedial amendment, modification or narrowing of such term would frustrate an essential purpose of the Agreement for one or both Parties, the Party(ies) so harmed by the invalidation of the term in question shall have the right to terminate this Agreement under Section 9(a) hereof.

This language highlights the difficulties of drafting around the issue, in this case requiring a judgment call, which might later be challenged, as to whether or not a term involves an "essential purpose" of the Agreement for one or both parties. It is likely better than nothing, providing a potential path toward termination, but it is still an uncertain path.

Perhaps the cleaner and better approach would be to provide, in appropriate cases, specific exceptions to the applicability of the *Severability* clause along these lines:

Notwithstanding the foregoing, the provisions of this Severability clause shall not apply in the event that any part of a Party's performance is deemed invalid or inoperative for any reason, in which case the entire Agreement shall be deemed terminated according to Section 9(a).

Severability clauses rarely deal directly with "frustration of an essential purpose" issues as explicitly as in the last two drafting examples. When faced with unusual *Severability* questions, the better approach is probably to try to address them clearly and directly elsewhere in the agreement, likely in close proximity to the potentially problematic terms or provisions themselves. This could involve providing for alternate terms or provisions in the event of invalidation, including specific rights to alternate or substitute performance, rights of termination or modifications to fees, as just a few examples.

In general, it is not necessary or advisable to overthink *Severability* issues. The three examples of *Severability* clauses above arguably became progressively clearer, with the third example probably being the best of the three. But having a general awareness of when and how to draft creatively to account for unintended consequences could prove useful in the context of legally or regulatorily uncertain performance requirements or remedies provisions.

Assignment

Almost every contract contains an assignment clause that looks something like this:

> *This Agreement may not be assigned by either party without the prior, written consent of the other party, which consent shall not be unreasonably withheld. This Agreement shall be binding on, and shall inure to the benefit of, the authorized successors and assigns. Any unauthorized assignment shall be void.*

In general, "the law" favors assignability, hence the need to specifically prohibit assignment if it would be undesirable. Always forbid assignment with language like the example above when (i) it is important to you that the other party itself perform their side of the deal and not otherwise sell or assign those commitments to a third party that might lack the special skills or resources required to competently and timely perform under the agreement, or (ii) you want to ensure the contract is not sold or assigned to a competitor or other concerning purchaser.

Important M&A Fix

The biggest point to consider with every *Assignment* clause is whether to include a clause negating the need for consent to assignment in the event of a merger or sale of your company – an "M&A" transaction. In the interest of making such transactions go smoothly, it is almost always a *very good idea* to add something like the following to an Assignment clause:

> *Notwithstanding the foregoing, no consent shall be required as to any assignment involving a merger, sale or reorganization involving all or substantially all of a party's assets or capital stock.*

If your company might be sold one day, add this language to every agreement that could be part of the sale. Having to obtain a lot of signed consents in the middle of a deal is very distracting and can result in substantial delays, increased legal costs, and unnecessary uncertainty. As all M&A lawyers know, delays and uncertainties can kill deals.

Additionally, each consent required to close a merger or sale transaction comes with the risk that the party whose consent is required will demand other commercial concessions in exchange for the consent, which can feel like a form of "commercial extortion." The important clause found in the above example, "*which consent shall not be unreasonably withheld,*" helps to remove some of this risk, but not all. The best protection of all is to remove the requirement of consent for mergers, sales or reorganizations.

The value of this "best practice" was reinforced for the author in a transaction when his client and a related company were being acquired in a multi-billion dollar deal. The author's client had more than one hundred active contracts. The related company had as many or more. The author had overseen all of his client's agreements and only three required consent to assignment – a lease, a banking agreement and a "cloud services" agreement with a global provider. The legal team for the related company had to spend more than a month chasing down consents for almost every one of its contracts. Needless to say, the author's legal work looked better in this deal.

Change of Control Language

Sometimes, a clause prohibiting any kind of assignment without consent will go the next step further and also prohibit a "change of control" without consent. This is most common where the party pushing for the language is concerned that the agreement will be transferred to a competitor in a deal structure not requiring any assignment of the agreement.

> *Assignment. The Distributor may not assign or transfer this Agreement, in whole or in part, by operation of law or otherwise, without the Company's express prior consent. Any attempt to assign or transfer this Agreement, without such consent, will be null and of no effect. For purposes of this Section, a Change of Control will be deemed to be an assignment. Subject to the foregoing, this Agreement will bind and inure to the benefit of each Party's permitted successors and assigns.*

Earlier in the same agreement under *Definitions*, Change of Control was defined as follows:

"Change of Control" means a transaction or a series of related transactions: (i) in which one or more related parties that did not previously own or control at least a fifty percent (50%) equity interest in the Distributor obtains ownership or control of at least a fifty percent (50%) equity interest in the Distributor; or (ii) in which the Distributor sells all or substantially all of its assets.

As the above language suggests, a "change of control" generally involves the sale or other transfer of a majority of a company's stock or other ownership interests, including by merger or reorganization. Contracts generally only need to be assigned in "asset sales" where the contract is being sold by one entity to another as an asset, but not in "stock sales," where the entity that is party to a contract will remain a party to the contract even after its capital stock changes hands.

However they are written, requirements for consents to changes of control should be resisted whenever possible, and certainly any time such a requirement might complicate or interfere with an advantageous M&A transaction. Sometimes through careful and persistent negotiation, the other party will agree to limit the applicability of a change of control clause to one or more specifically identified competitors.

In negotiating these issues, the best strategy is often to be upfront and firm that your company cannot risk losing a hugely important opportunity to sell the company by having to chase down a consent to a transaction that almost certainly will not be harmful to the other party, since the acquiring company will be fully and equally obligated to abide by the exact same contractual terms.

Governing Law, Venue and Jurisdiction

Governing Law, Venue and Jurisdiction clauses vary considerably in scope and specificity. The most basic versions are only one sentence:

Governing Law. This Agreement shall be governed and construed by the laws of the State of California, excluding its conflict of law rules.

This only covers which state's laws apply to the agreement, not where any disputes will be heard. Commercial agreements are generally more detailed and specify where lawsuits must be filed and which courts have jurisdiction. This example is more typical:

This Vendor Agreement shall be construed in accordance with the laws of the Commonwealth of Massachusetts excluding its conflict of law provisions. The parties agree that the sole and exclusive venue shall be in the state or federal courts located in the Commonwealth of Massachusetts, and each party hereby consents to the jurisdiction of such courts over itself in any action relating to this Vendor Agreement or the parties' relationship.

Here is an example of a governing law clause with additional bells and whistles.

This agreement shall be construed and enforced in accordance with the laws of New York, excluding choice of law. In any action relating to this Agreement, (a) each of the parties irrevocably consents to the exclusive jurisdiction and venue of the federal and state courts located in the State of New York, (b) each of the parties irrevocably waives the right to trial by jury, (c) each of the parties irrevocably consents to service of process by first class certified mail, to the address at which the party is to receive notice, and (d) the prevailing party shall be entitled to recover its reasonable attorney's fees, court costs and other legal expenses from the other party.

In general, the additional language in (b), (c) and (d) above all make sense as basic ground rules for any potential commercial litigation. Waiving "trial by jury" means that a judge would hear and decide any case, which can lead to faster, less expensive and more predictable outcomes in commercial disputes. The issue of "legal expenses" will be touched on again below under *Legal Expenses/Legal Fees.*

Governing Law Issues

In general, it is often best to have the "governing law" for an agreement be that of your own state, where presumably you have better access to local counsel who are knowledgeable about your state's laws.

But the advantages or disadvantages of one's home state laws are not always obvious and assessing them is difficult for non-lawyers. Some states have more advanced case law, particularly regarding complex business disputes. And in other states, statutory law can be potentially very helpful or very unhelpful to one's case.

It may very well be true, for example, that a California based company negotiating with a company in Washington might be quite agreeable to Washington law if California courts have already taken concerning positions in the same industry.

On the other hand, there might be statutory or case law reasons for preferring the laws of New York or Delaware, in particular, but also possibly the laws of Texas, Florida or Arizona, just to name a few.

Venue and Jurisdiction

Governing law is important, but the selection of venue and jurisdiction can have even greater tactical significance. Another state's laws *might* actually be preferable in a dispute, but you might not know that until there is litigation unless you first spend some time and money to discuss the issues with counsel from that state.

With venue and jurisdiction provisions, though, if the other party knows they can sue you in another state away from your headquarters, they immediately know this tactically valuable information:

- It will be more expensive and less convenient for you to litigate than for them.

- Litigation will require you to find and hire competent local counsel with no local conflicts of interest.

- You are unfamiliar with the state's case law.

- You are unfamiliar with the local court rules and customs.

- You are also unfamiliar the court system's reputation for speed and efficiency and the quality of the judges in the system.

Something non-lawyers do not realize is that litigating outside of your own state often doubles legal expenses. Local counsel knows the local court rules and customs but might not be willing or able to quickly get up to speed on all of the facts of your case, or even the controlling law. For this reason, most out of state litigants work closely with their trusted litigation counsel in addition to their local counsel.

When litigating outside your home state, local counsel usually files the pleadings and other documents and ensures compliance with all local court rules and customs, while regular litigation counsel, or "lead counsel," oversees local counsel, reviews documents, guides the litigation strategy and often even argues the case.

Negotiating Strategies re Venue and Jurisdiction

For these reasons, home court advantage is worth negotiating when the parties are from different jurisdictions. The party with the most leverage usually wins on this point, but sometimes it is the better negotiator. Here are some ideas for out-negotiating the other party.

First, for commercial arrangements where one of your template agreements is a reasonable starting point, and if your state has favorable laws and good courts, use language adopting your state law and providing for your local venue and jurisdiction. And do not give it up too easily.

On the other hand, if the other party is insisting on a venue and jurisdiction that could be disadvantageous, point out that a contract need not limit venue and jurisdiction to a single, specific place, push for striking all references to venue and jurisdiction, and suggest a governing law clause specifying the law of New York, Delaware, or another suitable, neutral state where one of the parties or the agreement has at least some connection.

If the parties are equal in negotiating leverage, it is logical to simply strike venue and jurisdiction provisions, in which case a suit could probably be brought in either party's hometown. As an important side-note, the courts of a state with jurisdiction can and will apply the law of another state specified in a governing law clause.

If these tactics do not work, another strategy is to suggest language requiring that either party filing a lawsuit must file it in the other party's hometown. While not ideal, this can level the playing field and discourage the other party from filing a dubious lawsuit.

When neither party seems willing to give up its preferred venue and jurisdiction, a final strategy is to suggest that both parties agree to a mutually inconvenient city with good courts, provided that it bears some relationship to at least one of the parties or to the agreement. If either party has offices or operations in the county in question or if part of the agreement is to be performed there, the legal requirements for venue and jurisdiction should be met.

Notices

Notice requirements can look innocuous, but they must be read and followed carefully, particularly when the objective is to reject inadequate performance, provide notice of an alleged breach, terminate an agreement, or provide notice of an indemnifiable claim.

Here is a typical *Notice* clause:

All notices, consents and other communications under or regarding this Agreement shall be in writing and shall be deemed to have been received on the earlier of the date of actual receipt, the third business day after being mailed by first class certified air mail, or the first business day after being sent by a reputable overnight delivery service. Any notice may be given by email or facsimile, provided that a signed written original is sent by one of the foregoing methods within twenty-four (24) hours thereafter. Unless a Party provides written notice to the other Party of a change of address, each Party's address of record for notices shall be the address provided by it on the signature page hereto.

And here is a *Notice* clause that takes a different approach to when notice is deemed received:

> *NOTICES. Except as otherwise expressly provided in this Vendor Agreement, all notices or demands shall be in writing, and shall be sent (a) by courier or in person with signed receipt, (b) by nationally recognized overnight delivery service, prepaid, with signature required or (c) by email (with confirmation of transmission), and in each case shall be sent to the other party at its address set forth in the Program Terms or to such other address or email address designated from time to time in accordance with this Section. Notices are deemed received upon actual receipt or refusal of delivery.*

Strict compliance with *Notice* provisions is important whenever *time is of the essence* for the communication in question. If, for example, a party wants to accuse the other party of breach and commence a cure period with a view toward trying to terminate an agreement, strict compliance with the *Notice* requirements is required to "start the clock." Overnight delivery to the correct person at the correct address is almost always a safe approach.

Notice of Non-Renewal

The same is true if a party wants to give timely notice of its intent to "non-renew" a contract that renews annually or on some other cycle. If the non-renewing party sends notice by email instead of sending a required mailing or overnight delivery, the contract in question will auto-renew.

As previously mentioned, the author knows of an unfortunate case in which an over-priced contract for commercial uniform services auto-renewed for a five year period because the buyer's attempted non-renewal communications did not comply with the agreement's *Notification* requirements. The economic impacts of this oversight were significant.

Address Updating

In addition to sending notices correctly, it is equally important to ensure you are receiving notices correctly. If official notices under a commercial agreement are going to the wrong place because you moved and communicated this incorrectly, you are still "deemed" to have received them and you are out of luck if important communications were missed.

When your company changes its mailing address, it is not sufficient to casually mail out generic change of address letters to everyone the company does business with using whatever addresses you think might work. Providing an effective "Notice of Address Change" under a commercial agreement almost always requires strict compliance with the *Notice* provision itself. *Notice* provisions vary widely and may require that notice be sent to the Chief Executive Officer, the Chief Financial Officer or to the General Counsel, and possibly to more than one such person at entirely different addresses.

Force Majeure

Force Majeure is Latin for "superior force." *Force Majeure* clauses spell out when and the extent to which a party's performance is excused temporarily if it becomes unable to perform its obligations *due to events beyond its reasonable control,* such as fire, flooding, war, civil unrest, natural disaster, or other specified events.

As with other common contract provisions that all start to look the same from one agreement to another, subtle variations can have significant unexpected implications, including potentially trapping a party for too long in an uncertain relationship and with uncertain remedies.

Here is a very basic example:

> *Force Majeure. Neither Company nor Reseller shall be liable for any delay or failure in performance arising out of acts or events beyond its reasonable control, including, but not limited to, fires, labor disputes, embargoes, impacts to or loss of cellular or other wireless coverage, requirements imposed by government regulation, civil or military authorities, judicial decisions, acts of God, or by the public enemy.*

While brevity is often a virtue, overly brief *Force Majeure* clauses like the above can be problematic if triggered. In this case, the non-performing party's obligations to give timely notice or to mitigate are unclear, as is the potential duration of its excused non-performance. This clause also says nothing about what rights, if any, the other party would have to end the relationship or take other action to protect itself.

The following example does a better job covering some of these details, particularly the underlined text:

> *Force Majeure. In the event that either party is prevented from performing or is unable to perform any of its obligations under this Agreement (other than a payment obligation) due to any act of God, acts or decrees of governmental or military bodies, fire, casualty, flood, earthquake, war, strike, lockout, epidemic, destruction of production facilities, riot, insurrection, materials unavailability, <u>except to the extent such failure was caused by the party invoking this Section</u>, or any other cause beyond the*

reasonable control of such party (collectively, a "Force Majeure"), and if such party shall have used its commercially reasonable efforts to mitigate its effects, and if such party shall give prompt written notice to the other party, its performance shall be excused, and the time for the performance shall be extended for the period of delay or inability to perform due to such occurrences. Regardless of the excuse of Force Majeure, if such party is not able to perform within ninety (90) days after such event, the other party may terminate the Agreement.

In this example, (i) the *force majeure* occurrence cannot have been caused by the non-performing party through its negligence or poor planning, (ii) the non-performing party has a duty to use commercially reasonable efforts to mitigate, and (iii) the other party has the right to terminate after ninety days. Among other things, this clause makes it clear, consistent with much of the case law, that the non-performing party is not excused simply because performance turns out to be more burdensome or difficult than anticipated.

Mutual Suspension of Performance

A buyer that would otherwise be burdened with ongoing payment obligations or other performance commitments might also add a mutual suspension of performance clause like the following at the end of the above example:

"During any period of delayed or suspended performance hereunder, the other party's performance obligations shall also be suspended and that party shall be entitled to a refund of any fees paid by it covering the period of the other party's non-performance."

Inappropriate Force Majeure Triggers

In addition to looking for missing provisions, it is prudent to look for items in the litany of *force majeure* triggers that do not belong. Both clauses above include references to labor difficulties, for example. As labor disputes, strikes and lockouts are within the ability of a party to prevent or timely end, the author generally strikes such references.

Drafters should be alert for other similarly questionable triggers that might find their way into a *Force Majeure* clause.

Economic Force Majeure

Neither sellers nor buyers should assume that a *Force Majeure* clause can be invoked in the event of a market crash, economic downturn, or other economic or financial disruption facing a specific industry or sector. The author helped defeat a claim of economic *force majeure* under a log supply agreement, winning a $240 million arbitration award against a global paper company that wanted to stop accepting logs during a prolonged slump in paper prices.

Economic *force majeure* is not recognized or accepted in the case law and buyers should be alert for and delete any listed force majeure triggers that might otherwise cloud that issue.

Entire Agreement/Integration/Merger

"*Entire Agreement,*" "*Integration,*" and "*Merger*" are three terms used for the same type of clause that essentially says "this is the parties' entire agreement."

Here is a typical clause:

> *The Client acknowledges the Client has read, understands, and agrees to be bound by this Agreement and further agrees it is a complete and exclusive statement of agreement between the parties which supersedes all proposals, oral or written, relating to the subject matter of this Agreement.*

This language should always be a reminder to consider (and ask others if necessary) whether there are any RFP (Request for Proposals) responses, side letters, email communications, oral assurances, or other sources of representations about the product, service or other expected or promised attributes of performance that should be incorporated into the document. Otherwise, this clause renders them unenforceable.

Legal Expenses/Legal Fees

Legal Expenses or *Legal Fees* clauses are not found in every agreement, but any party that believes it will generally be on the correct side of the law and the facts might consider regularly including something along the following lines in its agreements:

> *The substantially prevailing Party in any action arising out of or related to this Agreement is entitled to reimbursement of its reasonable lawyers' fees and expenses resulting from the action.*

This is commonly referred to as a "prevailing party" clause. Its purpose is to contractually re-write the common law prohibition against awarding attorneys' fees and other expenses in litigation. The words *"any action"* are sufficient to cover both litigation and arbitration.

A prevailing party clause substantially increases the financial risks to any party that might consider breaching an agreement opportunistically. Being reminded of the clause, such a party will have to think twice about breaching to force new concessions or to leave the other party in favor of a lower cost provider of similar services.

The threat of a potential attorneys' fee award gives the party with "clean hands" substantial leverage in any negotiations before or during litigation. More than once the author has issued warnings along the lines of *"I'm fine if you want to pay me to sue you to confirm how this contract should be interpreted."*

Prevailing party clauses are revisited in Chapter 8, *Dispute Resolution*.

Survival

Survival clauses spell out which provisions of a contract remain in force despite the contract's termination. These would normally include the following types of clauses:

- Payment of Fees
- Intellectual Property
- Confidentiality
- Representations and Warranties
- Effects of Termination
- Remedies for Breach
- Disclaimers and Limitations of Liability
- Indemnification
- Governing Law
- Venue and Jurisdiction
- Legal Expenses

A survival clause can be as simple as the following:

The following paragraphs of this Agreement shall survive termination: 5, 6, 7(a), 8, 10, 12 and 13.

More elaborate *Survival* clauses sometimes contain potentially helpful "catch all" language and may also deal with outstanding payment obligations and similar matters, along the following lines:

Notwithstanding the expiration or termination of this Agreement for any reason, (a) any provision of this Agreement that imposes or contemplates continuing obligations on a party shall survive the expiration or termination of this Agreement for any reason, including without limitation, the rights and duties of the parties under Sections 2, 6, 9, 13 and 14; and (b) all undisputed fees due and payable hereunder through the termination date in accordance with Section 4 shall be paid within thirty (30) days of the termination date.

Although disputes involving *Survival* clauses seem to be rare, it is always a good drafting exercise to make a check by all provisions in an agreement that should survive its termination and make sure they make it into the list of surviving clauses.

Authority

Authority clauses are often repetitive of similar statements found under clauses captioned *Representations and Warranties* and suffer from somewhat flawed logic, but they are nonetheless common and potentially valuable in the event of certain types of disputes.

Here is a typical *Authority* clause:

Each of the parties represents and warrants to the other that the execution and delivery of this Agreement and the performance of the obligations under this Agreement have been duly authorized by all requisite action of the governing body of the party, if any, and that the person executing this Agreement is fully authorized to bind that party.

The somewhat flawed logic in such an assurance is that the person signing on behalf of a particular company could be lying, in which case the company would likely seek to disavow the contract as unauthorized. That would not limit the rights of the other party to go after the individual who fraudulently signed the agreement, but that might be little comfort to the defrauded party.

This flaw is little more than an intellectual curiosity though. Each party to an agreement should always take reasonable steps to ensure that the person signing for the other party does in fact hold the proper title or role to bind that party to the agreement and to make the *Authority* representations and warranties enforceable against that party as its duly authorized officer, owner or agent.

Counterparts

"Counterparts" is a fancy word that means the parties may sign more than one copy of the same document or even separated signature pages. This language was particularly helpful when it was common for parties to fax signed signature pages to each other. Here is a typical clause:

> *This Agreement may be executed in one or more counterparts, each of which shall be deemed an original and all of which together shall constitute one and the same instrument.*

Notwithstanding the presence of a *Counterparts* clause in an agreement, once the necessary signatures have been obtained, including by electronically swapping signed signature pages, it is critical that one of the parties take responsibility for providing itself and the other party with identical versions of the entire agreement, with all required signature pages and all required exhibits, schedules, and attachments.

When parties simply swap signature pages without taking steps to assemble final, complete, fully executed (signed by both parties) copies of the agreement, there is a substantial risk that one or both parties is likely to be completely unable later to accurately confirm that both parties actually signed and exactly what they signed. This is a common and potentially costly mistake that is easily avoided with minimum effort, particularly with the use of electronic document signing platforms.

Signature Block

There are at least two points worth making about the *Signature Block*. First, as noted just above, it is surprising how often parties have difficulty finding their signed copies of agreements. Sometimes in the excitement of closing a deal, one party or the other fails to get a fully executed copy of an agreement or fails to properly file it away in a place where it can later be located.

Second, with respect to any important contract being signed by a subsidiary of a larger company, consider requiring the parent company also to be a party to the agreement. This can provide added insurance that the other party will perform and, if not, that you will be able to look to the more substantial assets of the parent to satisfy any damages available under the contract. This is an issue that needs to be identified earlier than at the signing stage, since large companies rarely move quickly to sign anything.

Chapter Six

IMPLEMENTATION

Signing and Filing

Ideally, each party signs two copies of an agreement so that each has a version with ink signatures. In the real world, more often than not, one party gets an original and the other gets a copy. Companies are also increasingly using electronic document signing platforms to manage the signature process.

Either way, it is important to get a final, fully executed copy, complete with all exhibits, attachments, and other documents referenced as being part of the agreement and file it in a safe physical or electronic location where it can be quickly retrieved.

As simple as this sounds, non-lawyers often think their job is done once they have signed an agreement and sent it to the other side for signatures. Follow up as many times as necessary to obtain a complete and fully executed version of every agreement. When dealing with larger companies, this can take days, weeks, or sometimes even months.

All fully executed contracts should be promptly escorted to a centralized filing system, ideally a secure and well-organized virtual data room. A redundant system of hard copy and electronic copies provides high availability and the best assurance against loss or destruction of your only original.

Tracking

When dealing with lots of contracts, it is important to establish (i) a spreadsheet, database or other system for organizing and tracking key information about a company's contracts, and (ii) a "tickler" system to provide timely alerts of auto-renewals and other deadlines.

The contract tracking system should capture and organize the following types of information for each agreement so key information about each contract (and groups of contracts) can be quickly and easily obtained without having to retrieve and read individual contracts repeatedly for the same information:

- Counterparty Name
- Counterparty Address
- Contract Title/Name
- Type of Agreement
- Effective Date
- Expiration Date
- Notice Period Required to Cancel or Non-Renew
- Next Notice Date
- Contract Amount(s)
- Internal Department
- Internal Legal Contact/Employee
- Miscellaneous Notes
- Limitation of Liabilities
- Insurance Requirements
- Assignability

A tickler system can be as simple as an entry in standard appointment software or it can be just one of many features within a fully integrated contract management software platform, as discussed below. Whatever system is used, it is important to ensure that the proper individuals receive timely notice of any performance deadlines, deadlines for non-renewing, contract expiration dates and deadlines for exercising options to extend.

Contract Management Technology

In recent years, numerous contract management software platforms have been developed and launched to handle a range of tasks relating to contracts. These systems boast varying functions and features, including automatically reviewing contracts, highlighting issues and suggesting language changes, facilitating red-lining and version control during negotiations, managing contract approval and signing, providing indexed and searchable storage repositories, and alerting contract administrators of renewal notice dates and performance deadlines.

As potentially useful as these systems are, they are relatively expensive and probably most suitable in the following types of circumstances:

- Companies with high volumes of contracts.

- Business activities prone to disputes, where reliably retaining every edited version of each agreement showing marked changes and editing notes would reduce those risks. Examples might include contracts involving construction and development, intellectual property licensing, joint ventures and mergers and acquisitions.

- Other circumstances where technology-assisted contract reviewing and contract administration features would be important to offset risks of mistakes and missteps due to poor contract drafting skills or weak internal administrative capabilities.

Testing one or more of these platforms on a trial basis would be the best way to determine the extent to which one might warrant the additional expense by providing drafting or administrative efficiencies, creating a more reliable record of contract negotiations, or otherwise reducing risks of drafting or administrative missteps.

Performance

Once a contract is signed, entered into a database and tickler system, and filed, the next important step is ensuring that both parties perform. In order to avoid disputes and to receive the benefits of your bargain, it is important to watch your own performance as well as the other party's.

Managing Your Own Contract Performance Problems

If you are unable to meet your obligations under an agreement, the best course is to get a signed waiver or modification from the other party as soon as possible. In situations where even a temporary waiver or minor modifications of your commitments is not enough, you should either exercise any termination rights you have under the agreement or negotiate a termination or major modification.

Any time a contract dispute could be looming, consider consulting competent counsel without delay. Unlike cheese or wine, legal problems rarely improve with age. *Dispute Resolution* is the topic of the final chapter.

Acknowledging one's own contract performance problems quickly and, where appropriate, looking for the best possible exit, might allow the other party to mitigate its damages. Acting quickly and in good faith also reduces or eliminates arguments by the other party that, in *bad faith,* you strung it along with false representations, knowingly hid serious problems, or caused it to futilely invest additional resources to its detriment.

As discussed in Chapter One, *Contract Law,* conduct that is dishonest or not consistent with the commercial standards of the industry might result in otherwise difficult to obtain punitive damages or awards of costs and legal fees on top of other successfully proven damages.

So when your own performance is the problem, fix it, get a waiver, get a modification, or seek a negotiated termination of the agreement if that is the best path for cutting both parties' losses. But do not do anything that will allow the other party to characterize you as dishonest, deceitful, or otherwise morally reprehensible.

Managing The Other Party's Contract Performance Problems

On the other hand, if it is the other party who appears unable to perform, this also cannot be ignored. Another party's poor performance should not be permitted to continue without either (i) a mutually signed written waiver acknowledging the performance shortcomings and providing for corrective actions within a stated timeframe, or (ii) written notice to the other party that it is in breach and that the breach must be cured within any stated cure period or rights of termination might be exercised.

Early Intervention

Although these are awkward communications that can strain relationships, non-performance issues rarely work themselves out. Without intervention and, left uncorrected, they often lead to bigger and more troubling problems. Early intervention conducted in a non-antagonistic manner is usually best, even when the issues are tough for both parties to acknowledge.

Missing an opportunity to document non-performance or to set rights of termination into motion often represents a painful lost opportunity, after which the parties' rights and obligations may become clouded, less certain, and more costly to resolve.

Tactical Termination or Renegotiation

It is also worth noting that another party's performance shortcomings sometimes provide a perfect opportunity to terminate an agreement for tactical reasons – perhaps a pivot away from an unprofitable business line, signing a deal with a more promising business partner for similar services, or just simply getting out of a bad agreement.

When value still exists in a relationship despite another party's shortcomings, another tactical possibility is to force a renegotiation of the contract. In these cases, review the markups exchanged during negotiations and look for the highest value concessions to try to force on the other party in exchange for a waiver of the performance shortcomings or a modification of the performance obligations.

Acting in Good Faith

It can be tempting sometimes in business to see tactical advantages in terminating an agreement based on inflated or poorly substantiated allegations of poor performance. As described in Chapter One on *Contract Law,* most jurisdictions recognize an *implied duty of good faith and fair dealing* in commercial contracts.

Claiming a clearly immaterial breach as justification for termination when the agreement really only allows for termination for material breaches could very well be found to violate this implied covenant.

Breach of contract claims, therefore, whether based on performance issues or other alleged violations, should be provable and made in good faith. Terminating an agreement for spurious reasons that will not stand up in court could backfire.

Deal Evolution

Sometimes business deals evolve over time beyond the parameters of what was originally negotiated. Be alert for this. Once you are operating beyond the "four corners" of your agreement, it becomes more difficult to pin down each party's rights and responsibilities.

This can have particularly serious consequences. For example, where new intellectual property rights are created, or where new potential liabilities to third parties could arise. Contractual arrangements should not be permitted to evolve materially outside the requirements of the written document. The parties should enter into as many written amendments or addendums as necessary to keep up with any such changes. Although it is best to not "open up" the entire agreement every time something immaterial changes, it is a good idea to consider whether other aspects of the business relationship have changed also or should change.

Amendments and addendums are the subjects of the next chapter.

Chapter Seven

AMENDMENTS AND ADDENDUMS

Amendments and addendums are similar types of documents except that the word addendum suggests merely adding new terms and amendment can mean both adding new terms and changing existing ones. Amendments and addendums alike need to be signed by both parties and responsibly filed away.

The term Addendum Is sometimes misused as a substitute for "exhibit," "attachment," or "schedule." By way of distinction, unlike an addendum or an amendment, exhibits, attachments and schedules do not need to be signed if they are properly "incorporated by reference" into an executed contract, amendment or addendum as described in Chapter Five.

Changing Circumstances

Contract amendments are very common in business relationships. Sometimes a relationship is going well and the parties want to expand it to cover more products or services. Sometimes the opposite occurs and a party no longer wants to offer a particular product or service and wants it removed from the agreement. Renegotiation of pricing terms is another common driver of amendments and addendums.

Changes can also be requested when a company is sold. An acquirer will often try to renegotiate some of the acquired company's outstanding agreements after the acquisition closes. The acquirer may want to add or drop lines of business, cut back on or eliminate redundant services, or simply conform contract legalese to its own standards.

Addendums

Again, an addendum is a document signed by both parties that *adds* something to an agreement – hence the first three letters "add." If an addendum changes anything, it should be pretty discrete. Otherwise, "Amendment" is probably the better document caption.

Addendums are commonly used to:

- establish a new price or fee schedule,

- add a new product or service,

- add a new territory or other license enhancement,

- run a special joint program, like a marketing campaign, or

- impose a new restriction or accommodate a new regulatory requirement.

Amendments - Contract Surgery

Whatever the reasons for a particular amendment or addendum, it is important to approach the task with reasonable care. Parties are often more cautious and deliberate with initial agreements than with subsequent modifications, an understandable but problematic tendency.

Contract amendments are a bit like surgery. Prior to an operation, the surgeon will look at the patient's charts, study their medical history, and talk with other doctors and family caregivers.

Before diving into a contract amendment, due care warrants reading the agreement and any amendments and possibly talking with others who more directly manage the relationship.

These steps are necessary to understand the current status of the relationship, what is driving the amendment, the details and scope of the amendment, whether the amendment makes business and legal sense, what areas of the existing agreement the amendment impacts, and the key business and drafting issues.

Almost any material amendment to an agreement essentially warrants going through a process that is just as deliberate as the agreement's initial negotiation and drafting, although hopefully on a more accelerated time frame given the narrower issues.

Tactical Considerations

Even where you or the other party may be thinking in terms of fairly narrow or minor changes, consider how those changes relate to the rest of the agreement and relationship, and whether or not other changes should be negotiated while "the patient is open."

These are tactical considerations that depend on the nature of the relationship, the nature of the proposed changes, the potential value of other possible changes, and the other party's likely response.

Based on the answers to these questions, a request for an amendment from another party could be an ideal opportunity to fix or clarify terms you are not happy with, or to add terms that were missed or that were previously beyond your negotiating leverage.

On the other hand, where the other party still holds most of the power in the relationship, sometimes the best approach is to agree to only very limited, "surgical" modifications. This is particularly true if other amendment proposals might cause the other party to push for disadvantageous revisions.

Consistency and Good Contract Management

Whatever changes are finally decided upon, they must be compared carefully against the entire original document for consistency. Are the correct defined terms used? Do you want the same or different standards applied to determine the adequacy of some new performance? Should the same penalties or rights of cure and termination apply for poor performance?

It is also important to keep contracts and related amendments very organized. Amendments should be chronologically numbered in their captions in a manner that makes it easy to establish the order of precedence of the documents.

In a virtual data room, an agreement and its amendments would hopefully look something like the following:

- Development, Hosting and Licensing Agreement Between Big Medical Device Company and Best Medical Information Data Service Company dated February 3, 2012.

- Amendment No. 1 dated July 22, 2014 to the Development, Hosting and Licensing Agreement Between Big Medical Device Company and Best Medical Information Data Service Company dated February 3, 2012.

- Amendment No. 2 dated May 3, 2015 to the Development, Hosting and Licensing Agreement Between Big Medical Device Company and Best Medical Information Data Service Company dated February 3, 2012.

- Amendment No. 3 dated February 3, 2018 to the Development, Hosting and Licensing Agreement Between Big Medical Device Company and Best Medical Information Data Service Company dated February 3, 2012.

Too Many Amendments

Sometimes a contract will accumulate two, three, four, or more amendments. This is not necessarily a problem, but the possibility of confusion is worth considering.

It is no big deal, for example, if all of the amendments cover similar, narrow pricing adjustments. But sometimes each of several amendments addresses different issues and touches different parts of the original document. Once an agreement has been amended three or four times with documents that each make two or three changes, it can become almost impossible for most readers to comprehend the agreement as an integrated whole.

When substantive amendments are stacked upon multiple other substantive amendments, the resulting cross references can get increasingly difficult to follow. The need to read multiple documents and double check numerous cross references can make it increasingly challenging to harmonize with the original agreement and the other amendments, leading potentially to drafting errors and disputes.

Even without any drafting errors, persons unfamiliar with the history of an agreement and its handful of amendments can struggle to make sense of the tangle of documents.

At this point, should you start over with a new, integrated document that harmonizes the original agreement and the amendments? This can take the form of an entirely new agreement or what might be called an "amended and restated agreement." The term "restated" means all of the agreement's terms are in the new document, which restates or supersedes the original and its amendments.

If the relationship is good and the other party is easy to work with, starting over on a fresh document can be the best approach. If the other party is difficult to work with, the end result might be worse than the risks associated with a confusing patchwork of amendments.

Chapter Eight

DISPUTE RESOLUTION

Commercial disputes are as varied as the companies, individuals, relationships, and subject matter involved in them. Disputes can be minor annoyances or company killers, and almost anything in between. Some can be handled through diplomatic efforts between CEOs or business owners. Others are sometimes resolved through negotiations following exchanges of *demand letters*. Those that cannot be resolved informally sometimes wind up in litigation or arbitration.

Experience is the best teacher when it comes to managing and resolving commercial disagreements, so qualified counsel should be consulted soon when troubles loom. Even when counsel is involved, though, non-lawyers familiar with a dispute should help shape and implement strategy.

Dispute Avoidance

Contract disputes can range from a series of difficult phone calls or terse letters to full blown litigation. They arise mostly over performance and payment concerns, but they can also involve issues around third party liability claims, other alleged breaches, and even tort claims outside of contract law.

Disputes are rarely profitable, except for the attorneys who resolve them. And the longer disputes last, the more costly and distracting they become.

Fortunately, contract disputes are largely preventable, as discussed in earlier chapters. When disputes cannot be prevented, it is usually best to resolve them on acceptable terms as quickly and efficiently as possible. That is the focus of this final chapter.

Be Right

As emphasized from the first pages of this book, dispute prevention starts at the beginning of any new relationship. Maintain the "moral high-ground" and the good graces of "the law" by doing things correctly: (i) promise only what you can perform, (ii) negotiate and draft good agreements, and (iii) perform what you promise.

Following this advice prevents disputes and it makes them easier, faster, and less costly to successfully resolve when they cannot be prevented. Short lived disputes arise sometimes even when the facts and law are on your side, but these are usually the briefest of distractions. Nothing takes the fight out of the other side faster than a "you should settle this" reality check from their own lawyers.

Keep Emotions in Check

The facts that give rise to any contract dispute, big or small, can be frustrating and annoying. When you pay for a product or service, you expect to get what you paid for. When you timely provide a good product or service, you expect to get paid.

Commercial disputes test the patience of most otherwise cool-headed individuals. Expressing anger, frustration, and other negative emotions is a logical and even reasonable response, but hostile emotions usually polarize parties, delay resolution, and detract from the end result.

Consequently, and perhaps counterintuitively, the hothead on the team is often not the best person to take the lead in dispute resolution – at least not in the early stages.

Disputes are Just Difficult Negotiations

The emergence of a commercial dispute is a bit like landing on the wrong space in the childrens board game, "Chutes and Ladders." Land on the wrong space and you slide backwards. When a commercial dispute arises, you go either sideways or backward, in either case, to a new "negotiation" phase of the relationship.

In almost any commercial dispute, the guidance in Chapter Three, *Negotiation*, is relevant once again, particularly the ideas in these excerpts:

> *Just like in poker and car buying, your demeanor, character and attitude all impact contract negotiation. In every negotiation, you should be*

professional, courteous and reasonable. In most cases, you will get more of what you want if the other party likes and respects you.

Continuing the poker analogy, negotiate in a consistently thoughtful, emotionally neutral and confident manner to avoid tipping your hand on issues of importance or weaknesses in your position.

The most productive way to avoid chatting too much to your own detriment in a negotiation is to get the other side talking and listen attentively. As we know, people love to talk about themselves and what is important to them. The more you let someone talk in a negotiation, the more they will probably like you and trust you, and the more you will learn about negotiating with them.

Listen for:

- Clues about what the other side might be willing to trade off.
- Issues they might stick on.
- Carrots you can throw into the deal to get more of what you want.

Yes, even in a dispute, it is helpful for the other side to like you – or at least not hate you. Personality types that cannot easily set aside emotions for tactical purposes are usually ill-suited to dispute resolution.

Initial Assessment

As noted at the outset, every dispute is different, including the players, the issues, the potential financial magnitude, and the range of options for resolution. The only feature common to most disputes is that the sooner they are over, the better.

Toward that end, it helps right up front to begin objectively and thoughtfully assessing the best path through the issues to the best possible resolution. Options can include one or more of the following:

- Playing down the issues and letting front line personnel try to work them out.
- Having the parties' respective CEOs negotiate in a series of calls.
- Exchanging demand letters and responses written by and possibly signed by counsel.

- Cooperatively engaging a third party mediator.

- Triggering contractually prescribed arbitration procedures.

- Filing a lawsuit.

Initially assessing which tools and strategies will bring the best result most efficiently is a bit like choosing golf clubs. Do not pull out your driver on the putting green just feet from the hole, do not pull out your putter in a sand trap, and do not tee off with your sand wedge.

The following discussion looks generally at a few key "clubs" in the dispute resolution bag.

Cats in Trees

When the author first hears of a simmering commercial dispute, the initial hope is that getting things back on track will not be much harder than getting a cat out of a tree. This analogy is instructive for assessing emerging disputes practically and non-emotionally. Here are some facts common to most real life cat-in-a-tree scenarios:

- Cats do not get stuck in high places out of malicious intent, it just happens sometimes.

- Any individuals involved, be they the cat's owners or concerned passers-by, are likely to be agitated and even difficult, including the cat.

- But eventually firefighters arrive.

- They bring no emotions or fears.

- Instead, they bring tools and problem solving skills.

- In the end, however scary the situation first looked, the issues are usually straightforward and most cats are retrieved unharmed.

- Then everyone gets back to business.

When a commercial dispute arises, see if it can be resolved quickly and informally.

- Do not be angry about the situation.

- Get on the scene quickly.

- Listen and learn.

- Defuse tensions.

- Use the lightest communications possible.

- Look for simple, mutually advantageous solutions.

- Try to resolve the situation quickly and equitably before the "cat" climbs higher in the tree, i.e., before frictions develop into a more full-blown dispute.

This softer, gentler approach is often ideal where the issues are relatively narrow, their potential impacts not too severe, and possible solutions or workarounds not too costly for either party. Examples might include a deliverable that is missing a minor feature or two, an operational misstep that has a small number of shared customers complaining, or a performance commitment that has been briefly delayed through error or oversight.

No matter how ugly a new dispute initially looks or sounds, a low-key, informal approach should always be considered before resorting to unnecessarily formal or hostile communications. Going back to the golf analogy above, it is important to recognize when a dispute can be resolved with a short, easy putt.

Even in situations where minor performance issues or other minor concerns are worked through by talking instead of exchanging letters or emails, it is probably worthwhile to document the resolution in a slightly more formal communication with the other party. This serves to: (i) create a record to share with the other party if issues arise in the future, (ii) document and define any performance "waiver" or other accommodation for future reference, and (iii) establish one's "good faith" conduct in the event larger issues arise.

Sand Traps

Occasionally, initial assessments reveal that a dispute probably is not going to be a short, easy putt, but more like a slightly messy shot, or three, from a sand trap – sand will fly, there will be a mess to tidy up, but hopefully the game is still salvageable.

There are often more options to consider in resolving disputes in the middle of the spectrum between easy fixes and low materiality on one end, and difficult fixes and extreme materiality on the other.

Disputes in the middle of the range can still be difficult and potentially costly for both parties, but there may be compelling reasons for not letting the situation deteriorate unnecessarily. These could include absence of viable alternatives to working with the other party, potentially serious impacts on customers or end users, serious regulatory concerns, or uncertainties around how liabilities might shake out in full blown litigation.

Again, the overarching goal of dispute resolution is to achieve the best result the most efficiently. This usually means exploring more cooperative and less threatening techniques first.

Sending in the CEOs

A tried and true approach to resolving moderately challenging but important commercial disputes is to coordinate talks between high level business principals, preferably the CEOs or owners in the case of two smaller or medium sized companies. Using high level principals often works well for a number of key reasons:

- They are unlikely to have been directly involved and can bring fresh attitudes and perspectives.

- Persons with broader responsibilities are more likely to see the bigger picture.

- They are more likely to be seasoned negotiators and deal makers.

- They have the latitude to make and enforce decisions.

- As company leaders, they are likely to take substantial pride in being able to solve problems.

The only downside to this approach, aside from distracting busy senior officers or business owners, is the possibility that the proposed solution to the dispute will involve completely unexpected concessions and compromises. When you send deal makers into a room, the end result is almost always a deal, and frequently it is a creative deal.

In the author's experience, once the initial surprise wears off and the ramifications of a deal negotiated by high level principals become clearer, it is almost always the case that the deal is a workable and acceptable solution that beats being in a dispute.

Principal-negotiated deals are rarely the resounding victories one might hope to achieve with a more litigious strategy given the right facts, but that is the tradeoff one expects for a result that is faster, cheaper, less distracting, and less damaging to the relationship.

Exchanging Demand and Response Letters

Sometimes it is not practical or advisable to have business principals try to work through a dispute. The other company might be too big, your CEO might be a bad negotiator, or the facts and issues might simply be too complex for anything but a demand letter.

A demand letter is simply a written communication from one party or its counsel to the other party or its counsel that usually (i) states the party's concerns, including providing notice of breach, as appropriate, (ii) requests specific actions and a written response, and (iii) possibly even hints at one or more courses of action that might be taken absent a timely and sufficient response. The art and science behind a proper and compelling demand letter clearly warrant involving legal counsel, if not to draft the communication, to at least look over your shoulder and watch for potential tactical errors.

Before writing anything, think about the communication's optimal achievable outcome. Then write to achieve that objective and exclude anything that is not necessary or helpful toward achieving the objective, such as any pointless venting.

Even in more serious situations, communications that are prematurely combative can harden positions and, more importantly, cause the other party to rush to the courthouse. Inadvertently prompting the other party to file a preemptive lawsuit or initiate an arbitration deprives you of the substantial tactical advantages of choosing the time and place for doing so.

While some attorneys recommend a more stern approach to demand letters, the author prefers what one might call "diplomatic corporate-speak" - language that is serious and clear, but also relatively dry and non-hostile.

Non-threatening corporate-speak for this style of correspondence might include words and phrases like *"concerned," "disappointed," "unfortunate," "unacceptable," "harmful," "causing substantial damage," "considering our options,"* and other somewhat benign language that is clear and firm, but not judgmental or overtly threatening.

Here are some other drafting considerations:

- Assume that all of your oral and written communications could come back to haunt you or help you in the event of litigation.

- Any written communication that offers settlement terms and that could be harmful if used as evidence in litigation should include the following all caps Federal Rules of Evidence notice: "FOR SETTLEMENT PURPOSES ONLY - F.R.E. 408 COMMUNICATION."

- As discussed in Chapter Six, Implementation, comply carefully with all notice requirements in the agreement.

- Avoid misstating any facts or otherwise creating further confusion.

- Err on the side of brevity to ensure that the other party's focus is on the right issues and to avoid compromising peripheral or additional claims one might make in the event of litigation.

- Preserve other claims and factual assertions with catchall phrases like "in addition to other concerns," "without limiting other claims we may have," and "among other issues we are still investigating...."

A demand letter will usually either elicit a formal written response or a request for talks. Any request for talks should be accepted and should be taken seriously as an opportunity to resolve the dispute before more expensive and more risky formal dispute resolution processes become unavoidable.

Mediation

In cases where demand letters and responses have been exchanged and the parties still are not making progress toward a mutually acceptable resolution, many attorneys and *alternative dispute resolution* advocates would suggest mediation. Mediation simply means paying a third party to play an objective and neutral role to guide the parties toward a mutually acceptable resolution.

In the author's limited mediation experience, mediators are often *too neutral*. Unlike a judge or arbitrator, they seem uninclined to bring their special knowledge or even informed opinions or judgements into the process. Instead, a common approach seems to be simply repeating back to each party the other party's positions, without helping the parties weigh or evaluate the positions.

This approach is more geared toward getting the parties to "split the difference," regardless of the true equities of the dispute. This is fine in cases where both parties' positions have merit, but it is potentially less useful to a party with a strong case and substantial damages.

Professional mediators would no doubt take exception to the above generalizations, perhaps rightly so. But these are legitimate issues to consider and ask questions about when considering mediation or a particular mediator. When interviewing a mediator, consider asking how he or she deals with situations when the facts and law clearly favor one party's position – is he or she willing to point that out to the other party and, if so, how firmly?

Code Red – Zero Sum Disputes

At the more extreme end of the spectrum are the riskiest and potentially most costly disputes. These sometimes involve what might be called a "zero sum game." In a zero sum game, mutually advantageous solutions are less likely because one party's potential wins usually correspond to direct potential losses for the other party.

The following are examples of more serious disputes where one or both parties face material risks of financial damages, losses, and other harms:

- A party rejects the performance of the other and refuses to pay.
- A party's performance has clearly fallen short of expectations but that party says the performance was good and insists on being paid.

- A party falsely claims breach by the other and tries to improperly terminate an agreement against the other party's protests.

- A party falsely claims force majeure and stops performing.

- An expensive data breach occurs and both parties blame each other.

- A consumer product is the subject of a governmental recall order and each party blames the other for the defect.

As a cautionary "heads up," disputes like these frequently trigger requirements to notify insurance carriers, especially the last two bullets above. Failure to provide timely notice of potential claims against an insurance policy can result in complete or partial disallowance of the insurance coverage. When major disputes arise, insurance notice obligations and other insurance issues should be top of mind, including the possibility of nudging the other side to notify its carrier where appropriate, or even providing direct notice under an "additional insured" rider.

Get the Facts

The first step in any potentially serious dispute is to gather all of the facts, including all documentation and records. Understanding the facts from both parties' perspectives helps reveal any potential options for compromise and how to pursue them.

Collect and Protect Records

Warning: all records gathered, including emails, meeting notes, and other written communications, will be subject to discovery by the other side in any litigation. They and all other potentially relevant records must be protected from destruction if litigation is likely. Knowlngly or negligently destroying records during or prior to litigation is a terrible mistake with potentially severe penalties.

In-house law departments protect potentially important litigation records through what is often called a "records hold" process, including internal communications that describe the records to be exempted from routine records destruction processes and how they are to be handled until further notice.

Discovery Issues and the Attorney-Client Privilege

While investigating any dispute, be cautious about creating new records, particularly timelines, notes or journals, fact summaries, summaries of conversations, investigative reports, or electronic communications of any kind. All documents not created by an attorney are discoverable in litigation.

Letting an attorney create all new documents, on the other hand, helps keep them out of opposing parties' hands via the attorney-client privilege and the attorney work product doctrine. Hopefully it goes without saying that inadvertently sharing key information about your case with the other side can be harmful in litigation.

Anytime potential disputes arise, team members should be strongly cautioned against making written statements of any kind reflecting judgments, legal conclusions or improper motivations regarding the facts or issues. Opposing counsel have wide latitude under litigation discovery rules to search through all available physical and electronic records. Loose statements that can be taken out of context or otherwise turned against their creators are always prized targets of such searches.

Bill Gates and Microsoft famously learned this the hard way in the late 1990s while defending anti-trust litigation brought by the Department of Justice and Attorneys General of twenty states. In defending allegations that Microsoft had competed unfairly in the Internet browser space, Mr. Gates was forced to explain away awkward and unhelpful internal communications such as *"We need to continue our jihad next year. ... Browser share needs to remain a key priority for our field and marketing efforts."*

Use of Counsel

In dealing with situations that are more likely to end up in litigation, arbitration or other formal dispute resolution processes, consulting with counsel before proceeding further is highly advisable. But exactly *how* to use counsel is a different tactical question.

Early in a dispute, counsel can help make sense of the facts, compare them to the terms of the agreement, and objectively assess the strengths and weaknesses of the parties' positions. But when and how to involve counsel in communications with the other party is a trickier tactical question.

Keep the Lawyers behind the Scenes as Long as Possible

When one side gets lawyers involved, the other side will almost certainly do the same. In fact, attorneys are prohibited from "communicating with parties known to be represented" by other counsel, so it is often impossible to involve lawyers in formal communications without automatically triggering the involvement of the other side's counsel, particularly where two larger companies are involved.

Importantly, although you get to select your own counsel, you do not get to select opposing counsel. If less-experienced or combative counsel become involved, options for a reasonable resolution can be materially limited.

For these reasons, the author's preferred approach in many situations is to stay behind the scenes initially, help frame the issues and guide the strategy, but allow the principals to talk directly to explore potential solutions.

That does not mean written communications are not also important for providing notice of breach, responding to the same, or otherwise protecting one's interests, but they should not be written in a manner that precludes more informal communications between the parties' business principals.

Competent principals often have better success at negotiating solutions to complex commercial disputes without lawyers present. When they come to an "agreement in principle" to resolve a dispute, there are usually details to work out and sometimes the compromises seem more generous than necessary, but speed to resolution can be fast.

There are certainly times when it is better to put counsel out front in a dispute. Sometimes, for example, a letter from counsel is the only way to get a larger company's attention. A letter from counsel might also be more effective if the subject matter is legally or technically complex, if the other party is being extremely difficult despite having a weak position, or if regulatory concerns are involved. In these cases, it is sometimes more appropriate to lead firmly with a letter on counsel's letterhead.

Be Decisive

If initial communications and efforts to resolve a dispute seem unlikely to progress satisfactorily, and reasonably stern demand letters have gone unanswered, it often pays to be decisive. Letting issues or concerns drag on unaddressed sends the wrong signal to the other side. It can also lead to tactical disadvantages if the other side takes action first to file a lawsuit or arbitration demand.

The first question to address is what alternatives are provided under the agreement. Do you have a clear right under the agreement to terminate? To withhold payment or other performance? Does it make sense tactically to terminate or otherwise stop performing or is it important to continue to perform based on the nature of the dispute and the terms of the agreement? Again, these are questions that qualified counsel may be able to answer better than non-lawyers.

Suit for Breach, Declaratory Judgment Action

Few commercial disputes are worth litigating. But when litigation is one of the last tools left in the box, an unexpected law suit can be surprisingly effective at driving a positive outcome. The following "declaratory judgment" litigation strategy works best when several facts are present:

- The agreement requires or allows venue and jurisdiction in your town.
- The facts, the agreement, and the law are on your side.
- You have good litigation counsel.
- The agreement contains a "prevailing party" clause for attorneys' fees.
- Ideally, the other party is in a different city and state.

What is a DJ Action?

When the above factors are aligned, hitting the other party with an unexpected declaratory judgment action is sometimes all that is needed to bring them to the settlement table. A declaratory judgment action, or "DJ action," is a lawsuit that can be filed after one or both parties have begun "saber rattling" by sending notices of breach, demand letters or other communications evidencing a dispute.

In a DJ action, the plaintiff who files the suit will describe the dispute, including any unsuccessful efforts to resolve it, and request that the court issue a judgement "declaring the rights and obligations" of the parties and awarding appropriate damages. Contract disputes make up a meaningful percentage of DJ actions filed.

Courtesy Copy Prior to Filing

One element of the author's preferred strategy in using DJ actions involves sharing the draft lawsuit with the other side just hours before filing it. Again, this strategy is particularly effective when you can claim a hometown jurisdiction advantage by filing first, the facts and law are on your side, and you have a good litigator behind you.

This aggressive but often successful strategy usually plays out along these lines:

- Demand letters have been sent to or received from the other side of a contract dispute or other matter.

- Meaningful efforts to resolve the dispute have been made and documented.

- A draft "Complaint for Declaratory Judgment" is prepared, often also including specific claims for damages for breach of contract, claims for attorneys' fees and other costs, and any other applicable claims.

- Beyond the typical litigation legalese, the draft complaint will detail all of the facts warranting relief, no matter how unflattering to the other side.

- On the morning that the complaint is to be filed in the local courthouse, a "courtesy copy" is sent electronically to counsel for the other side, with a note that the complaint is being filed in the coming hours and including an offer to discuss.

- Opposing counsel often calls within the hour.

There are multiple aspects of this strategy that help to drive quick and favorable outcomes.

- It puts the other side and its counsel in a very time sensitive situation, with imperfect information and the threat of an imminent tactical setback.

- Although nobody likes to be caught off guard and forced to make important decisions quickly, counsel is left with little choice but to call.

- Sending the courtesy copy just hours from filing ensures that the other side will not be able to file a competing complaint first in another jurisdiction, but it does give the other party a brief window to prevent the filing by resolving the dispute.

- One of the incentives for not letting the suit actually be filed is the possibility that it will be seen and read by others, potentially harming the potential defendant's reputation as a commercial partner or competitor in the particular industry or sector.

- By selecting the venue and jurisdiction most convenient and least expensive for itself and gaining the upper hand in "telling the story" to a court, the party threatening the DJ action is generally in firm command of the tactical high ground, at least for the time being.

- The other side's motivation for a quick resolution will be all the greater if the agreement includes a "prevailing party" clause and it has the weaker of the two positions.

In the author's experience, once a courtesy copy of a well-drafted complaint has been received by opposing counsel, it usually is not long before requests to talk are received. If the parties can be brought together the same morning to try to resolve the dispute, the dispute can often be wrapped up the same day or within days.

Sometimes the other party's principals will be unavailable to weigh in on the emergency settlement talks and opposing counsel will ask for a delay in the lawsuit's filing. This can be agreed to, but only if the other party agrees in writing in a formal "standstill" agreement to not file its own lawsuit first.

In the event a standstill cannot be negotiated, the better approach is often to file the suit, while agreeing to *hold off on serving the complaint* for a few days while the parties negotiate. Although the lawsuit will still become a matter of public record, not formally serving the complaint gives the other party additional time to respond by not starting the 20 or 30 day clock for filing an answer.

This is definitely hardball, but where the facts warrant it, it is a tactic that often delivers excellent results very quickly. Of course, one always has to be prepared for the possibility that the other party is not going to back down. As a tactical matter, some recipients of a DJ action understand that they could improve their negotiating position by filing a formal answer and at least feigning interest in putting up a strong defense.

But if the facts and law are in your favor and you also have the hometown advantage, a prolonged, aggressive response to a DJ action is unlikely.

Made in the USA
Coppell, TX
01 February 2021